ADVANCE PRAISE

"*Brian has done us all a favor by capturing key points of his marketing wisdom and putting them in this book. Of course, it's more than just about marketing; it's insight into what drives decision making in a world that is hungry for authenticity.*"

—KATHY KOLBE, FOUNDER AND GLOBAL
THOUGHT LEADER, KOLBE CORP.

"*Do you know what you stand for? Are you clear on the core beliefs that drive your organization? If you don't, it's unlikely you'll achieve the kind of extraordinary success exemplified by the world's most beloved and high performing brands. Brian's book is an invaluable resource that will help you gain clarity around your core beliefs and ultimate Purpose. Highly recommend it for anyone seeking to cultivate a deeper, more meaningful connection with those they serve.*"

—HALEY RUSHING, CO-FOUNDER AND CHIEF
PURPOSOLOGIST AT THE PURPOSE INSTITUTE

"*I've had the pleasure to see Brian speak, work with him on my own speeches, and now read his book on how to build a brand. He is a master storyteller, so even when he's teaching you something, you feel like you're being entertained. After you finish* Stand for Something, *you will, indeed, be able to stand for something and build a brand people will be drawn to because of its authenticity and uniqueness. Don't walk. Run to the counter (or your online shopping cart) and buy this book so you can read it immediately.*"

—GINI DIETRICH, FOUNDER AND AUTHOR OF *SPIN SUCKS*

"*I've seen Brian's work firsthand. His approach and the outcomes he produces provide tremendous value to even the most talented marketers.*"

—ANDREW RAZEGHI, FOUNDER OF STRATEGYLAB, INC., EDUCATOR AT KELLOGG SCHOOL OF MANAGEMENT AT NORTHWESTERN UNIVERSITY, AND AUTHOR OF *BEND THE CURVE: ACCELERATE YOUR STARTUP'S SUCCESS* AND *THE RIDDLE: WHERE IDEAS COME FROM AND HOW TO HAVE BETTER ONES*

"*Brian is the one who taught me how brands truly connect, and why so many miss the mark. Open this book to any page and you'll see (and feel) why I believe in his message.*"

—ANDY CRESTODINA, TECHNOLOGIST, ENTREPRENEUR, AND AUTHOR OF *CONTENT CHEMISTRY: THE ILLUSTRATED HANDBOOK FOR CONTENT MARKETING*

"I say this with 100% confidence and clarity: Brian Burkhart will challenge everything you've ever known about building a company that matters, and there is no one in the world better to write this book than him."

—ROBBIE ABED, EXECUTIVE GHOSTWRITER, MARKETER, AUTHOR, AND CONTRIBUTING WRITER FOR *INC. MAGAZINE*

"In an era where it's all about the architecture of the brand, Brian's book couldn't be more timely."

—JOHN ONDRASIK, PLATINUM RECORDING ARTIST, GRAMMY-NOMINATED FOUNDER OF FIVE FOR FIGHTING, AND KEYNOTE PRESENTER

Alex-

STAND FOR SOMETHING

MAKe
WAVES!

BRIAN BURKHART

STAND

FOR

SOMETHING

THE POWER OF BUILDING A BRAND
PEOPLE AUTHENTICALLY LOVE

LIONCREST
PUBLISHING

STAND FOR SOMETHING

The Power of Building a Brand People Authentically Love

ISBN   978-1-5445-0258-8 *Paperback*

        978-1-5445-0259-5 *Ebook*

Interior illustrations created and designed by Kaylee Conrad,
except "Da Coach," which was illustrated by Ron Burkhart.

This book is for anyone willing to stand for something. Together, let's make some waves.

And to Shawna, my favorite person on the planet: You are the love of my life, the reason it's all worthwhile.

CONTENTS

INTRODUCTION

THE MOST VALUABLE
REAL ESTATE ON EARTH

It's the best advertisement I've ever seen.

When I first saw it, I thought to myself, "I don't know who's responsible for this, but I need to give them a hug." The TV commercial wasn't impressive because of any fancy special effects or in-your-face messaging. What made it remarkable was an incredibly simple and all-too-rare phenomenon:

The company prioritized their core beliefs and then shouted them, loudly, throughout the entire commercial.

Here, let me paint a picture for you:

The year was 2014, and Subaru had just rolled out its

new marketing and advertising campaign for their fully redesigned Forester model. The commercial I saw was an integral part of that campaign. The one-minute spot is called "Backseat Anthem," and, let me tell you, it lives up to its name.

"Backseat Anthem" begins just like every other car commercial: with shots of a beautiful car quickly snaking down a curvy forest road (remember the name: Forester). Then the scene cuts to the empty backseat of the car with trees zipping by in the background.

A deep, reassuring voice cuts through the quiet din of the uplifting music. "The humble backseat," the voice says. "It's the first place most of us ever sat. The place we trust to hold our most precious cargo."

The next shots are of grandparents and children buckling themselves into the backseat, a father putting his newborn baby into a car seat, and a dog sitting in the back with his eyes glued to the great outdoors.

Then we hear the line that is the crux of the campaign and what makes me admire the commercial so much:

"We believe the backseat can be the most valuable real estate on Earth. That's why we designed our newest Subaru from the backseat, forward."

The whole commercial lasts all of one minute. But in that short amount of time, Subaru shows what feels like the entire spectrum of human experience, from birth to old age, all taking place in the comfort and safety of the backseat of a Forester. The commercial is designed to make the Forester look and feel like a protective bubble. And Subaru creates this experience by focusing on their core beliefs, not facts and figures.

At no point during "Backseat Anthem" does Subaru mention the Forester's cost, estimated gas mileage, torque-to-wheel ratio, the variety of colors it comes in, the softness of the interior leather, or even the new features that make the car safer than its predecessors. Subaru doesn't say, "The Forester is only $28,000." Instead, they say, "We believe the backseat can be the most valuable real estate on Earth."

Do you *feel* the difference?

Now, if you're in the market for a new car, and you believe in protecting your loved ones, you know for a fact that your beliefs match up with Subaru's. You hear their message and think, "You know what? Maybe I should check out this new Subaru Forester, no matter the cost."

CORE BELIEFS: THE HEART OF YOUR ORGANIZATION

Core beliefs are at the heart of every organization, whether those organizations realize it or not. Subaru did what most organizations won't: They not only discovered their core beliefs, but also shouted them out loud in a profound way that's easy to communicate and even easier to understand. They stand for something. The process they executed so effectively in their new campaign is the heart of what connects people to companies.

And it's what will make people fall in love with yours.

I don't care what kind of organization you run. Whether it's a nonprofit, huge global enterprise, small private company, or even a government agency, if humans built it, there was a reason they put it together. That reason is the heart of the organization. It's more than a vision for the future, and it's certainly more than a mission statement. It's a core belief, and it's why your company exists.

Imagine a business that people are almost magically attracted to. A business where people line up for your latest products, regardless of price, feature, or service. Imagine reading cover letters from job applicants begging to work with you because the company *spoke to them* on a level they've never experienced before. Imagine selling your services even though you barely mention who does the work, how it's done, what it costs, or what your experience is.

That's the power of knowing your core beliefs.

The brands that people love the most, including Nike, Disney, and Apple, have the most concretely defined core beliefs of any companies in existence.

Nike's Core Belief: Bring *inspiration* and *innovation* to every athlete* in the world.

Disney's Core Belief: We believe in creating world-class stories and experiences for every member of the family.

Apple's Core Belief: We believe that people with passion can change the world for the better.

*If you have a body, you're an athlete.

Core beliefs are how we align ourselves not only to the companies we work for and run, but also to the companies we buy from (and even the political parties we associate with).

Yet most companies don't nail down their core beliefs. In fact, most companies don't even realize they should. They don't inspire customers, employees, or anyone else for that matter. Nobody hears these companies' names and says, "I love them." Still, there *is* a reason these companies exist, and their founders *did* believe in something when they first started them. The problem is that these companies' core beliefs aren't clearly defined. Nobody has put them into words.

And if they're not put into concrete, relatable words, then the core beliefs don't exist.

The most loved companies stand for something—and they shout it out over and over again. Subaru nailed it with "Backseat Anthem." And so can you.

WE BELIEVE IN MAKING WAVES

The company I spend the most time at, SquarePlanet, is smack dab in the middle of the Arizona desert. We don't have a preponderance of water, so you won't see many waves anytime soon. At least not of the aquatic variety. Yet our core belief is "making waves."

The waves we make involve helping our clients discover their core beliefs and then elevating them, so people can remember *and* act on them. When people act from their core beliefs, it almost always causes trouble and disrupts their industry. That's how *they* create waves. At SquarePlanet, we've helped all kinds of people, including executives from Google, United Airlines, Citibank, Coca-Cola, Northern Trust, and Jim Beam, as well as eight successful *Shark Tank* contestant teams, define their core beliefs and create waves in the process.

Here's the secret, though: Nobody cares what you or any of those major companies actually *do*. In fact, when people ask you what you do, and you answer by *actually saying what you do*—such as IT consultant, sales leader, or carpet cleaner—you are being selfish. Seriously! When you answer in this way, you're thinking about yourself and how you appear. But people don't connect with *what* you do. They connect with *why* you do it.

This is why when people ask me what I do, I tell them: "I make waves."

We're wired to answer the question of what we do by explaining *only what* our work entails, but my goal with this book is to help you see that *why* you do what you do is what truly connects people to you and your company.

HEARD OVER THE HERD

Maybe one exists, but I've never heard of someone teaching a class on how to find your company's core belief. No one forces you to fill it out on your tax forms or include it in your firm's marketing materials. That's why I wrote this book: to help you see how important it is to find your company's core belief and actually stand for something.

> Ask everyone you know and you'll get a lot of blank stares. The vast majority of people have no idea what they believe, what they stand for, or what, in the long run, they're working for. For most people, we just do life, but we're not fully immersed in our beliefs.
>
> Oh, and BTW, if you think it's only about money, you're wrong. Every day, people give up high salaries to work for companies whose core beliefs align with their own. Seriously. It's a thing.

I want you to have an actual purpose for waking up every day, rather than just putting one foot in front of the other, like a herd animal.

In fact, for millennia, humans have taken advantage of this herd mentality in other animals. One of the best examples is located in what is now known as Buffalo Jump State Park in Gallatin County, Montana. For at least 2,000 years, Native American tribes flocked to that river valley for one purpose: buffalo hunting.

The tribes strategically lured herds of buffalo toward the cliffs of the valley by planting vegetation all the way to the edge. Then, when the time was right, designated runners worked the herd into a frenzied stampede, directing them toward the deadly precipice. One by one, the frightened buffalo would follow the momentum of the herd until all of them had careened to certain death.

This hunting strategy relied on one simple principle: Buffalo will always stay close to their herd. They feel most comfortable keeping their heads down and feet moving forward within the confines of the pack.

And it costs them their lives.

The same phenomenon occurs every day in the business world. Those who follow the crowd go off the cliff. Those who go their own way can thrive in greener pastures.

THE STATUE IN THE MARBLE

Now, I want to be clear about something: I cannot tell you exactly what your core beliefs are. I'm just good at helping you *discover* them.

Michelangelo said that every block of stone already had a statue inside of it. It was his task as the sculptor to reveal what was already in the stone. Similarly, I want to chip away the stuff that's hiding your core beliefs and reveal what's already there.

This book will give you a methodology—rooted in numerous case studies—to find the core beliefs already hiding in the proverbial marble of your company. It will also give you best practices for implementing your core beliefs in your hiring processes, company messaging, and brand strategy. These will help you become more efficient with your time and energy by focusing on the most valuable people: those who already share your core beliefs.

Whether you're recruiting employees or customers, you'll never have enough bandwidth to successfully reach everyone. You want to reach the people with similar beliefs, and the only way they'll find you is if you identify your own beliefs and stand for them at every turn. That's how you get heard above the herd and keep yourself from galloping over the cliff. That's what Subaru did so well in "Backseat Anthem," and that's what I want you to do after you read this book.

I never did get a chance to give that commercial creator a hug. I don't even know their name. Frankly, your customers may never meet you in person and may not know your name, either, but by standing for something, you can create a brand people authentically love.

Your core beliefs hold a sacred spot in your company's operations, and sometimes an even more sanctified place in your customers' psyche. That is truly the most valuable real estate on Earth.

Are you ready to find your core beliefs?

PART I

CORE BELIEFS, DEFINED

CHAPTER 1

NOT WHAT OR HOW, BUT WHY

"Determine what behaviors and beliefs you value as a company and have everyone live true to them. These behaviors and beliefs should be so essential to your core that you don't even think of it as culture."

—BRITTANY FORSYTH, VP OF HUMAN RELATIONS, SHOPIFY

Imagine your business lost half a billion customers in just over six years.

Heck, imagine if you even had a half-billion customers to lose! That would be pretty devastating, wouldn't it? But that's exactly what happened to McDonald's between 2012 and 2018. Why did they lose all of those customers? Because their customer base doesn't know what the company stands for.

Look, don't get me wrong—I've got tremendous affinity

for McDonald's. Over the years, I've done a ton of work with them. And some of the biggest lessons I've learned come from dealing with the Golden Arches. I even worked at their famous global training facility, Hamburger University, for four years as a gameshow host (sometimes it's best to not ask)! McDonald's and I go way, way back. So with that affinity comes some tough love.

They sell deep-fat-fried, greasy french fries and not-made-to-order cheeseburgers on the same menu with the McFit salad featuring fresh leaf lettuce and mandarin oranges, and now, all-day breakfast. I look at that menu and say, "What are you?" They call it fast food, but it's not even fast anymore. Last time I was there, I thought, "This is taking forever!"

And this. What the heck is this? It is NOT a fake image. I know, because I personally took the picture of this huge billboard in Chicago's River North neighborhood. Is this a bakery item? A dessert item? A lunch item? Do you guys bake all of a sudden? WHAT ARE YOU, McDONALD'S?!

I'm hard-pressed to come up with a single, clearly defined statement of what McDonald's believes. That's their fatal flaw: They believe that everyone should be their customer. That leads to inconsistent and incongruent messaging (Carrot McMuffin, anybody?). As such, customers like me have a muddled picture of who they are and why they do what they do.

The point is, nobody can fully engage with your company if you aren't clear about your core belief.

NUMBERS *DO* LIE

With McDonald's, numbers don't tell the whole story. Specifically, their stock price. You can look at their earnings and their stock price and say, "Look at that—they're doing great!" But once you dig deeper, you see that they're covering up larger problems. They've had massive global expansion, which has fueled their growth and makes everything look rosy.

But if you divorce their international growth from their domestic growth, you get a different story: They're languishing in America.

The problem is fixable for McDonald's: If they stopped trying to be everything for everyone, they'd have more time, energy, and money to make it work. If they just said, "You know what, we're an indulgent, ridiculously tasty place to get a cheeseburger, fries, a shake, and a Coke," their sales would likely go up because people who love those items would authentically *love* McDonald's.

START WITH WHY

Simply put, your core belief is whatever you believe in and stand for. Most fundamentally, your core belief is *why* your organization exists. Right now, you don't have the words for your core belief.

As a business leader, it's vital that you actually take the time to stop, question, and wonder why you do what you do to discover your core belief.

Just trust me on this, find eighteen minutes and watch Simon Sinek's TED Talk, "Start with Why." It's consistently one of the most popular TED Talks ever. In it, he explains the concept of core beliefs. He says that your customers don't care *what* you do. They don't care *how* you do it. What they care about is what you stand for and *why* you exist.

Once you become clear with that, it galvanizes everything within your organization.

You can do amazing things all day long, but if you don't know why you do them, or where those behaviors come from, then you'll go through life blind.

Again, this is not about what your company does, or how you do it, and it's certainly not about your mission and values.

> For example, if you value driving results, that's great—that's part of the equation of what your organization wants, but it's not who you are at a deep, DNA level. You don't *believe* in driving results. I mean, who's for driving a *lack* of results? Driving results is a WHAT, not a WHY.

The point is, if you get the *why* right, your customers will figure out the *what*. I'll reference the "Backseat Anthem" Subaru commercial again. If you believe that the backseat is the most valuable real estate on Earth because you transport your children back there, then all of a sudden the red paint and caramel-colored leather interior—the *whats*—just kind of come together, because you got the *why* figured out first.

Our brains are wired to have deeply held beliefs (which we'll talk more about in Chapter 2), but you most likely don't challenge your beliefs or even consider why you hold them. So if you can tap into them and get clear on what you believe, as well as find others who believe the same things, you're in business. You'll not only attract more talent into your company, you'll also attract the right kind of clients: the ones who love you.

Confused yet? Yeah, this stuff is hard, I know. But stay with me…we'll get there, I promise. As we explore a bunch of examples, this will all start to make sense.

THE KEY ELEMENTS THAT DEFINE CORE BELIEFS

AUTHENTICITY

There's no doubt about it—you have to be authentic. I can't say I believe in making waves and then go out and shy away from causing some trouble. I have to be the guy to say what no one else is willing to. I have to come up with an alternative idea, not just the first, most obvious one. If I'm not, then people sniff out that inauthenticity—they call BS.

United Airlines learned about inauthenticity the hard way. Way back in 2003, United created a new, low-cost carrier called TED, fashioned after the Southwest model. Frankly, it was a tragic misstep from minute one. All they did was rip out the first-class seats on 56 existing Airbus A320s, slap on a coat of paint with a new logo, use the same gates, same ticketing agents, same flight attendants, same pilots, same ground crews, and same everything else—then lowered the price. They even fashioned their in-flight food after Southwest's. The problem? The underlying financials just didn't make sense.

I was getting on flights out of O'Hare for 200 bucks knowing full well that six months ago they were charging me $800 for the same flight. How was that supposed to work?

The customers loved the lower prices. Great. Good for them. But what the customers didn't see was the underlying reason the Southwest model works: consistency. They only have one type of plane—the 737—so pilots, flight attendants, and everyone else can interchange any flight at any time, no problem.

United's fleet is a hodgepodge chock full of Boeings, Airbuses, Bombardiers, and everything in-between. Trying to structure it the same way just didn't work.

More than anything else, the venture never came close to

profitability, because they weren't authentic to who they were. United's commercials, website, and branding all cater to businesspeople, who care about schedule, not the infrequent travelers looking for price deals. Most of the corporate types you routinely see on United flights don't care about price. Cultivating price-centric travelers for an airline built to compete on schedule-centric business travelers was doomed from the outset.

United was not authentic to who they were, and authenticity is the No. 1 element to defining your core belief. What does it mean to be authentic? Easy: it's being true to who you are, not who you *wish* you were. And people sniffed United's BS from 33,000 feet away.

How do you find your authenticity? Start by looking to your founding.

FOUNDERS' STORIES

For startups, this is an easy task: Your founder probably works less than 20 feet away from you, so you can just walk up and ask them the story behind *why* they founded the company.

It's much harder if you work for a well-established firm— the founders might be long expired and forgotten. For example, HP aren't just a couple of letters on the front of a high-rise in Palo Alto, California. There were actually two men named Bill Hewlett and Dave Packard who had core beliefs about what their company meant and a well-defined reason why they started it.

No matter how far removed from your founders you are, you can look to their stories for a lesson on why your company exists and find the essential clues to your company's core beliefs.

TIESTA TEA: LIVING LOOSE

I love this story! Two childhood buddies happened to be studying abroad in Europe at the same time. One was in Milan, and the other was in London, so they decided to find a few cheap airfares (not on TED, mind you) and meet in Prague for a weekend.

Old pals from their Pee Wee baseball days, Dan Klein and Patrick Tannous spent a lot of time catching up in a street café in the Czech Republic's capital city. It was too early in the day to knock back beers, and a little too late to suck down coffee, so they did what the locals were doing and ordered a pot of loose leaf tea. No sawdust-filled paper bag on a string here—this was legit!

When the tea came out, they were mesmerized by the ritual of the experience—the way the cups were arranged, the specific way the waitress steeped and poured it, all the way to the intention with which they sipped it. It smelled heavenly, and they could even see little pieces of actual leaves unroll and unfurl with all their natural colors. It was ceremonial.

It was like nothing they'd ever experienced in the United States. Until that moment, tea had been a known but fully unknown commodity.

But there, in that Prague café, it was a beautiful sensory experience.

Patrick and Dan looked at each other and had the same idea: "Why don't we do this in the US?"

Eventually, they both went back to the States and their respective universities. From dorm rooms, they ordered their own loose tea leaves to create unique flavor profiles. Things got real when they entered a business competition, got some money, worked tirelessly, and caught a few big breaks. Today, they are the co-founders and gurus behind Tiesta Tea, a company worth roughly $20 million and available in over 7,000 retail stores, including Target and Costco.

Through all of their ascension to success, they held onto the belief that drinking tea should be a ritualistic experience—a ceremony. Tea was something to be savored, not rushed.

Before that moment in the Prague café, they'd always perceived tea drinking as a hoity-toity experience only for the elites, not the masses. But it was such a unique and enjoyable experience, they decided to make it accessible to everyone. As such, each of their products is easy to understand and identify. The labels call attention to the desired effects of drinking the tea blend (think *immunity* or *energizer*), *and* the names of the tea blends are spectacular: Cocoa Mint Chill, Blueberry Wild Child, and Kiwi Cherry Bonanza, just to name a few.

None of this is by chance. It's all by careful design and based on the core beliefs of the business as a whole. The Tiesta Tea guys *could* put their loose tea in bags, but they won't. They *could* use fancy words, but they don't. Instead, they stick to their core beliefs and it resonates with those who believe the same things: that drinking tea is a fun, accessible, enjoyable ceremony, meant for everyone.

SPANX: MADE TO LOOK GOOD, NOT FEEL GOOD

Sara Blakely, the founder of Spanx, is the first female self-made billionaire manufacturing entrepreneur in the US. Sara started as a copier salesperson in Atlanta when she developed the first Spanx product. Her goal was to help people lift, form, shape, and fit their body into their clothes.

The garments are more than just a pantyhose, a girdle, or a slimming outfit—each item is a highly effective combination of all three.

She knew her Spanx products were valuable, but she faced an uphill battle getting them manufactured and distributed. Luckily, she did not stop until she got her way. She believed that women would want a product that made them look great in their clothes. She went to clothing mills and manufacturers, most of whom wouldn't give her the time of day because she was nobody to them. Not to mention she had little money and less experience. Through her doggedness, and the undying commitment to her beliefs, she eventually got an order from a single, major department store. The rest, as they say, is history.

This initial breakthrough was the opening she needed. Spanx is now ubiquitous—they are everywhere and on seemingly everyone. Spanx has expanded its lineup of body-shaping products, even creating a few products for men. Why do they do that, you ask? Because the core belief hasn't changed: Sara and the Spanx team want to create an undergarment that makes *people* look good in their clothes.

I get asked to speak at meetings and conferences all the time. And like many people, I'm more than just a little vain—I'm a lot vain! In an attempt to look good onstage and counter my flabby, middle-aged belly, I can admit it: I've tried the Spanx undershirts for men. They cost about $60 per shirt and feel great in the box, but once on, they require an Indy pit crew to remove them. It's like entering a wrestling match with a roll of duct tape. Expect rotator cuff surgery if you attempt to remove the shirt all by yourself.

Remember, the core belief of Spanx is to help me look good, not make me comfortable.

It's very simple: If you want to look good, buy Spanx. If you want to be comfy, buy Fruit of the Loom. Sara had a unique core belief, and that core belief helped guide her through times of uncertainty. That's the power of a core belief: It's a guiding light through stormy, uncertain seas.

DISTINCTIVENESS

In addition to being authentic, your core belief can't be generic, vanilla, benign, or safe. Here's a simple test: If you develop core beliefs that could apply to any organization, then they're not distinctive. Let me be clear here: to build a brand people actually love, you have to stand for something and break from the herd.

I can't tell you how many millions of khaki pants-wearing, Honda Accord-driving people pull up every day to work at a nameless, faceless, generic, safe, benign organization.

It's not inherently bad or wrong, it's just the same as those buffalo from the Introduction—following the herd, one foot in front of the other, until they go over the cliff to their metaphorical death.

To get the best talent, the best clients, and the best prospects, you better stand out and be distinctive. Otherwise, you risk, well, everything.

> SquarePlanet's main brand color is orange. Think nacho-cheese, traffic-cone, highlighter-marker orange. We use it everywhere. From the walls of our offices to the laces of my shoes, we embrace orange. Orange is the color of contrast—we very intentionally want to stand out. We want to be remembered. When we wear orange, it's not marketing spin—it's authentic to our beliefs and thus our brand. That's distinctiveness.

ASURION: ACTUALLY HELPFUL

There's a fairly decent chance you know the work of this global leader, you just may not realize it. In simple terms, Asurion is a cellphone replacement service. Yes, these are the kind people that talk you off a ledge when you ruin your $800 phone after accidentally dropping it into the toilet at a Justin Timberlake concert. They are the ones who get you a new phone in 24 hours and replace all your emails, pictures, and music.

At the helm today is a guy named Tony Detter. I'm jealous of Tony. He's wicked smart, good-looking, obviously athletic (played baseball at Stanford and, unlike me, does not need to wear Spanx for men), worldly, and perhaps more than anything else, charming. The man is amazing.

But when I first asked him about his company's core beliefs, I saw anything but amazing.

We act with integrity.

We are one team.

We drive results.

We deliver service excellence.

Sitting in Tony's office, I asked him, "What are Asurion's core beliefs?" He produced a beautifully designed print from a famous Nashville printmaker, framed and mounted under glass. The above words were perfectly typeset. None of it was inherently wrong, or something he should have been embarrassed about. It was all just so safe that there was nothing to lean into. It wasn't a belief; it was a series of words that almost any firm could have provided.

What you really want is something simple, but that you can also rally around. It's hard to rally around, "We drive results."

We got to work helping Asurion develop their core beliefs. Again, when we do this work, we don't seek to give companies anything that's not already there. We are only unearthing what already exists.

Like all of our clients, we did interviews with their team and asked them copious quantities of leading questions. Then we looked at their marketing presentations, their onboarding materials, and anything else that would give us an idea of what the organization was all about.

What we gleaned from the conversations with Tony and his team was that Asurion is *actually* helpful. They talked about how when you lose a phone, for most people it's like losing an organ. "Oh crap, my kidneys are gone! How do I get them back?"

Please, under no circumstances should you venture down a dark alleyway to haggle with a black-market kidney dealer. Instead, go to Asurion.

Tony and the Asurion team jump through hoops, help restore data, and get your phone FedExed to you the next morning. I remember one team member told me the story of a customer losing his phone, which had the last video of his grandpa before he died. It was a priceless memory that he had lost.

The customer was devastated.

The gang at Asurion helped retrieve the lost video. They saved that customer and his most precious memory of his grandfather, and that's pretty darn special.

So like chipping away at stone to find a sculpture, we found what was already there underneath all the superfluous corporate mumbo jumbo: that their 18,000-plus associates all want to make people feel whole again with their devices and data intact.

A core belief of being *actually helpful* is more true than, "We are one team." They don't hire new associates by asking, "Do you believe in being one team?" They hire new associates by asking, "Tell me about a time you were actually helpful."

Tony recognized that their current core beliefs weren't terrible or wrong, they just weren't anything anyone could get psyched about. Because of that awareness, he had the opportunity to galvanize his company. He made the courageous decision to change, and that is something to admire.

Are you willing to change? C'mon, you can do this!

LET YOUR CORE BELIEF GUIDE YOUR *WHAT* AND *HOW*

Greenspring is a financial services organization whose goal with every client is to provide them with clarity about their financial life.

The founding partner, Josh Itzoe, wants people to look at statements for their 401(k), their mutual funds, and their stocks, and understand exactly what they mean. He wants us to fully understand what all those numbers, charts, and transactions mean.

We helped him realize that his organization's core belief was to make his customers' financial lives clear and transparent.

Once we codified that belief, we wanted the notion of clarity to permeate everything in the organization. We wanted everything to be *clear*. So instead of getting black or opaque coffee mugs, we suggested they order clear glass mugs. Ditch the solid wood conference-room table and opt for a glass-top option instead. Walls? Tear them out—let's get some big windows instead, please.

Potential clients could sit down at the glass table with a freshly brewed cup of coffee in a clear Greenspring mug, and Josh could say, "We believe in clarity so much that the table, room, and even the coffee mug are all clear. Oh, and here's my clear business card."

It might sound gimmicky, but these seemingly superficial aspects have teeth. Take the HR department, for example. Josh could authentically ask them to only hire people who have the ability to speak in clear, easy-to-understand language, not just financial jargon. They want clarity in thinking, speaking, *and* in their environment.

This pervasiveness of clarity tells the people around them that clarity matters, and if someone wants to be associated with Greenspring—whether as an advisor or as a customer—they should respect clarity in all things. That means if some guy with a Stanford MBA comes in and just wants to crunch numbers and not worry about how he communicates with clients, Greenspring won't hire him, no matter how qualified he is. Because he doesn't fit the core belief of clarity.

LUSH COSMETICS: SO GOOD YOU COULD EAT THEM

Lush Cosmetics are the stores you can smell from 200 feet away. Their products are four-to-five times the price of a regular bar of soap you'd buy from Target, but they focus everything they do on natural and clean products, not chemical-based products. They package everything in super minimal paper packages, and blast their core beliefs all over the place. This includes their website and certainly on the walls of their stores. Lush believes in clean, clear, and natural products. If you share those beliefs, you'll pay the extra money—trust me.

For people who believe their body is a sanctuary and slathering unpronounceable chemicals all over your skin is a lousy idea, well then Lush is for you. And they'll spend more money to shop there. Lots more.

There are very few businesses that don't need to worry about the underlying cost structure and ultimate selling price of their products. Typically, these are super premium brands that move small amounts of a few very expensive things. Think Ferrari, Harry Winston, etc.

Lush isn't worried about competing on price. They realize soap, bath bombs, lotions, and other similar products are perceived differently by individual people. Person A may happily slap any old shampoo on their head, while Person B will **only** use organic, natural, paraben-free, goat-milk-derived, almond-essence, lavender-scented, hand-formed, free-range egg soap. Person B is a Lush customer, price be damned.

Core beliefs aren't HOW you do business, they're what you stand for.

YOU DON'T MEMORIZE CORE BELIEFS—YOU INTERNALIZE THEM

When Tony showed me the framed print with his original core beliefs for Asurion, I grabbed it from him. Then I hid it from his view.

"OK, say them to me now," I said.

He's a smart guy, oozing with IQ points. He got it, but it took a good, long time to go through the mental gymnastics of remembering those core beliefs.

"Tony, this isn't something you should strain to remember. If your core beliefs are real and authentic, they will be a profoundly deep part of who you are, and it will permeate every part of your being. It's not something to memorize. It should flow very naturally."

Your core beliefs are not marketing spin, and they aren't what or how you do something. They are the reason why your business exists—and that inherently means they're pretty darn important.

ZERO TO 60 IN ABOUT THREE DAYS

My father-in-law, Mike, is truly one of the manliest men in the world. He can fix anything, he's tough as nails, he owns literally every tool you can buy, he flies planes, and can pop wheelies on dirt bikes. He's everything I'm not. I'm a soft marshmallow of a guy and unfortunately for Mike, he got stuck with me as a son-in-law.

In spite of our many differences, we not only get along quite well, we actually like each other. Which makes it both funny and ironic that he makes his living producing oil—as in he owns and operates actual oil wells. He drives humongous four-wheel-drive trucks that he can rebuild completely on his own if necessary. I drive a hybrid (which can go zero to 60 in about three days, if you're rolling downhill), and I might be able to add wiper fluid if you really pushed me. I make my living dreaming up ideas, talking a lot, and more or less staying clean while sitting at a desk.

We have very different beliefs about lots of things—one in particular is fossil fuel use, as you might imagine. Neither of us is inherently wrong. Beliefs, like a fingerprint, are a most personal thing. Each of us has our very own, and not everyone is always going to agree—even those you may be quite close with.

Mike believes in high-octane power. He likes burying the gas pedal and moving fast! He believes in the roar of an internal combustion engine and conquering the muddiest of oil-field roads.

I send my shirts to be cleaned and pressed every week, I

have a collection of Japanese woodblock prints, and my car has never been off an asphalt surface.

Look deeper for a moment and you'll realize that a very key concept is buried in the differences between my father-in-law and me: Your beliefs lead to your actions.

We'll pursue this further in a moment, but for now, think of someone you know who dislikes their job. Oh sure, there are lots of reasons why, but I'm willing to bet you that one big reason is because what they believe as an individual is different from what the organization believes.

For example, at Greenspring, if you don't believe in open and honest customer service, you'll struggle.

Or if you run McDonald's and you try to appeal to everyone, you'll lose half a billion customers.

Remember, most entities don't have a clue as to why they exist, what they believe, or what they stand for. It's hard to find why your organization does what it does, and act in alignment with those beliefs. It's OK to be flummoxed— you're caught between a rock and a rock! But this book is giving you permission to struggle, be frustrated, revise, and most importantly, think about your core beliefs.

Generally speaking, people don't stop to think about this

stuff, so when you do, it might reveal that you're either not following the right path, or you're working in the wrong place. That's OK. But once you have that knowledge, act on it. Do something about it!

This book will help you navigate that space.

CHAPTER 2

THE COGNITIVE PSYCHOLOGY OF CORE BELIEFS

"Your beliefs become your thoughts. Your thoughts become your words. Your words become your actions. Your actions become your habits. Your habits become your values. Your values become your destiny."

—MAHATMA GANDHI

What I'm about to tell you in this chapter might sound like opinion, hearsay, or just another marketing tactic. I don't blame you. It's truly unbelievable. But stick with me anyway—I promise it'll be worth it.

Let's start here:

Beliefs are *not* actions—but there is a clear, causal relationship between the two. Your beliefs *lead* to your actions. In the largest context, that's what this thing called cognitive psychology theory dictates.

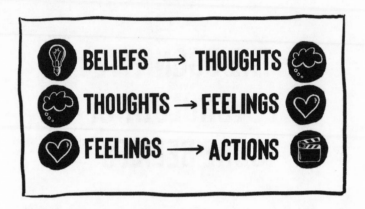

Just the other day, I ran this exercise on a live audience of about 500 people. I picked out a big guy named Calvin from the crowd and said, "OK, Calvin...whether it's true or false, just play along with me—you hate sushi. Terrible stuff. Absolutely gross. Got it?"

Calvin had the look of a meat-and-potatoes kind of guy.

"OK, sushi. Hate it. Got it."

I walked off the stage, right up to Calvin and said, "All right, you're in charge. This afternoon, we're all going out to lunch. All of us. And Calvin, you're picking the restaurant. What's the likelihood that we're going out for sushi?"

Calvin gave me a suspicious look, then said, "None."

"Exactly right, sir! If you believe sushi is awful, slimy, nasty raw fish, the last thing you'll say is, 'Hey gang, let's grab some spicy tuna rolls.' Instead, you'll say, 'Let's go grab a pizza or some cheeseburgers. Maybe barbeque. Anything but sushi.'"

It may seem like a silly example, but the key point is a big one: Beliefs lead to actions. A lot of people think beliefs and actions are equal, but they aren't—it's a causality, not an equality.

> A really contentious example—and no, this is not a political book, just an example—is the Second Amendment. If you believe the Second Amendment is incredibly important, then there's a higher likelihood that you'll have a gun. But if you believe that guns lead to a lot of horrific deaths, then your belief will lead to your actions—you won't have a gun. Think about it: How many anti-gun people own firearms? Not too many.

BELIEFS TO THOUGHTS, THOUGHTS TO FEELINGS, FEELINGS TO ACTIONS

There's a pathway in cognitive psychology by which beliefs lead to thoughts, thoughts lead to feelings, and feelings lead to actions. Therefore, you can draw a line directly from beliefs to actions.

But that line is not straight, nor easy to follow—it's like a corn maze. There are tons of twists and turns between beliefs and actions, and it's hard to see the endpoint from the beginning—but if you look at it from a high level, the pathway is clear.

Now, granted, it's difficult to see your beliefs—that's why you're reading this book—but it's quite easy to see your actions. So, if you simply reverse engineer your actions, you'll see your beliefs at work.

There's a lot of real science behind this idea *now*, but for centuries people could only intuit that beliefs lead to actions. Even Plato, way back sometime around 380 BCE, suggested that the brain was the seat of all mental processes. (Yes, I'll speak for Plato.) Nothing happens by pure chance—your actions don't happen randomly.

For example, if you're Plato and you believe your body is a temple, you'll feel committed to your health and wellness, which will lead to the action of daily physical fitness.

Plato didn't wake up one morning, hit the weights, deadlift 345 pounds, then hit the showers and say, "Fitness is for me." No. He said, "I think I want to feel better and live at peak physical fitness, so I'll work out."

A quotation from the journal *Frontiers in Psychology* sums it up nicely: "Every action that we take is grounded in an elaborate web of beliefs and goals."

After he hit the gym, where would Plato go for his protein shake? I gotta imagine he'd drop by the CVS on his way home. Here's why...

CVS: "WE DON'T SELL TOBACCO...WANT CHEETOS INSTEAD?"

Several years ago, CVS drugstores made a bold decision: They pulled more than a billion dollars from their bottom line. Why? To hold steady to their core belief that public and individual health is incredibly important.

What did the Woonsocket, Rhode Island-based retailer do? They pulled tobacco products off their shelves.

(Yeah, I'll admit it, that was a useless fact. I just wanted the word "Woonsocket" in my book.)

Although they knew Walgreens, their largest competitor, would hang on to an extra billion dollars of revenue CVS wouldn't access, they pulled tobacco anyway. CVS decided they would be hypocrites to espouse public and individual wellness and still sell products that cause heart disease, lung cancer, and general poor health.

> *Belief*: Public health is paramount.
>
> *Thought*: Tobacco products are harmful to health.
>
> *Feeling*: It's wrong to contribute to a negative impact on health by selling tobacco products.
>
> *Action*: Pulling all tobacco products from their stores.

But here's the dirty little secret...

Walk up and down the aisles of a CVS and notice what you see. Is it loaves of gluten-free bread? An all-organic produce section? Or hormone- and dairy-free milk substitutes? No. You see coolers full of beer, soda, and other brightly colored, sugary drinks. You see entire aisles of chips, cheese puffs, and other salty snacks. You see box after box of candy. Basically, you see a plethora of items that gravely impact people's health.

The decision to pull tobacco at CVS is a conundrum for me. I'm of the belief that most people will see through it and say, "Check out the chip aisle and tell me you care about people's health." But in theory, many others will say, "Oh, cool—CVS doesn't sell cigarettes. Let's go there." They lost a lot of revenue opportunities on this decision, but they also started a huge conversation, which has led to a lot of free advertisement.

They may have lost money in the short term, but they also

got a lot of people to rally behind their brand because hate it or love it, they stood for something and shouted it out loud. For that alone, go CVS, go; you're my kind of people. Now, excuse me, but where are those king-sized bags of Peanut M&M's, please?

WHICH WICH: GIVING LOVE THROUGH SANDWICHES

If you don't know this brand right now, you will. It's growing fast, including international expansion into places as far-flung as the United Arab Emirates. Branding master Jeff Sinelli started the Dallas-based sandwich company called Which Wich in 2003. And even though he's constantly on the go, he's always eager to discuss the founder's story for his company.

Ever since his upbringing outside of Detroit, Jeff has believed in making sandwiches with love. His grandmother, a Polish immigrant who spoke broken English, lived off of the small amount of money she had. As such, the best way for her to provide love to her grandkids was to feed them. Most of the time, she made cheese sandwiches for little Jeff and the others, made out of actual government cheese. If he was lucky, he might get a peanut-butter-and-jelly sandwich, but that was a special treat.

So when he grew up, Jeff built Which Wich on the

foundation of that special connection of love through food—specifically sandwiches.

I know Jeff. He's a great guy, but he's realistic. He'll be the first one to tell you that he's got a lot of competitors in that space because, frankly, making and selling a sandwich is nothing inherently difficult or special. Subway, Jimmy John's, Jason's Deli, Firehouse—the list goes on and on. Heck, you could even go to most grocery stores and get a custom sandwich right now. But in *none* of those restaurants do you get the experience you get at Which Wich: the feeling similar to your mom or grandma making you a meal as a means to declare their love. So he makes sandwiches like grandma would make: with heaping piles of high-quality ingredients, leaving you full, fat, and happy, just like you feel when you leave grandma's house.

Jeff didn't stop there. He realized that more people than you might imagine go hungry every day. In fact, Jeff will tell you that one in seven Americans is food insecure, meaning they're unsure of where and when their next meal will come from. Simple math informed Jeff that a lot of people couldn't afford the love he offered.

To take care of these people, he created a foundation called Project PB&J. He wanted to tap into that moment of growing up, when coming home from school and eating a PB&J could transport us to a warmer, safer place. Now, at Which Wich stores, when you pay for your own PB&J, you're also buying one for a hungry person. Additionally, Jeff leads "spreading parties," where corporate clients with a few hundred people get in a big ballroom, with music jamming and beers flowing, and make *thousands* of sandwiches that they distribute to local food pantries and homeless shelters in their area. It's awesome. And easily the best thing I've ever experienced in the world of corporate team building and charitable giving.

It all ties back to this idea that Jeff doesn't believe his company just serves sandwiches. They also serve love.

It's not hard to imagine how many people latch onto that belief that food is love, and remember those moments coming home from school. So damn right they'll contribute to the foundation and help spread the love. That's the power of standing for something and shouting it out loud.

Belief: Making sandwiches with love.

Thought: There are a lot of people who go hungry.

Feeling: We want to care for them.

Action: Project PB&J makes a massive number of sandwiches for food banks and shelters.

ALTEREGOAV: MORE THAN JUST THE FALL GUY

The corporate audio visual (AV) production business is awful. Oh sure, it's one of the coolest jobs on the planet if you do rock-and-roll concerts. But the corporate side? Hot garbage. It's the same technology, same gear, and often the same people, but somehow the worlds are perceived as vastly different.

If you've ever been to a decent-sized corporate event at a hotel, convention center, or any other kind of meeting space, you know that the AV production teams are *always* the fall guys. Whether a PowerPoint file is wrong, a sound system doesn't work, or, I don't know, a pack of wild dogs chewed through the power cord overnight, it's always the fault of the AV guys. Typically, these are actually hardworking people with good intentions, but frequently they're looked down upon as the occupants of the lowest rung on the totem pole.

It's odd, too, because these people are the backbone of meetings, and people still don't appreciate them. People often look at AV teams as the problem, but they're a solution—not just a bunch of grunts. Think artisans and skilled people with tons of experience executing highly technical tasks in a difficult environment under a lot of pressure.

How do I know so much about this? Because I'm one of

these people! A few years ago, I co-founded an AV production company. My business partner, Brian (yes, we're both named Brian), and I built a company called AlterEgoAV with the core belief that we want to transform the way people think about and experience AV.

For a moment, consider the last conference you went to—the one that was booked in a huge hotel ballroom. Just hours before the first keynote speech, that ballroom was a completely empty box. There was nothing in it except maybe some tables and chairs. The AV team had to turn that box into a theater, complete with lights, screens, a sound system, and other technology so you and your friends could see and hear what's going on. They *transformed* that space in a short amount of time for the audience.

From that single, foundational thought about the typical process, we created a series of beliefs that led to specific actions at AlterEgoAV. Let me say that again.

We created a series of beliefs that led to specific actions. Got it? OK, cool.

In the theater and AV world, there's a term called "show black," meaning the clothes one wears are all black. The idea is to blend into the background; you aren't to be seen or heard. You're just an invisible human who pushes a few buttons to fix a problem and off you go. Recall Brian and I had a core belief around transformation. We said, "No, we do not want to blend into the background. In fact, we want people to know *exactly* who the AV techs are."

That way, if their laptop's not working, if the projector fries a light bulb, or if a microphone simply dies, they don't have to search for a semi-invisible person specifically trying to blend into the background. Most presenters are in a highly emotional state already; why make it worse with AV issues?

Our solution, while simple, is rooted in our core belief: ditch show blacks for the exact opposite—neon green. Transform the old approach into a new, more robust one.

We outfit our AV techs in blazing neon green, so that at any point in a gigantic convention center with thousands of people running around, you can easily spot a tech when you need one. Additionally, we drop professionally designed and printed, full-color laminated cards on every lectern, in every breakout room with this message, "Have a problem? Call Dave." Dave, our lead tech, is pictured along with his mobile phone number. When someone calls Dave with an issue, they'll get personal assistance instantly.

People hear this methodology and they say, "Amazing.

Our people don't want to search for some no-name guy in black. I want to work with you, Dave, and the guys in green shirts."

Yeah, we know. It's because we started with our core belief.

Now, consider your organization. What actions can you take—even one as simple as changing the color of a shirt from black to green—based on your core beliefs to better connect with customers?

Belief: The power of transformation.

Thought: AV techs are typically hidden from view.

Feeling: We want to stand out to customers to transform their experience.

Action: Scream "Here we are!" with neon-green shirts, extreme niceness, and tech name reference cards.

HOW CODIFIED ARE YOUR CORE BELIEFS?

In our companies and in our personal lives, our beliefs are not often well-known—even to ourselves. Despite the companies I highlighted making conscious decisions based on their beliefs, most organizations and most people don't really think about the deeper underpinnings of where their actions come from. That means they're open to the influence of expectations or social norms.

You've seen it a thousand times: When people get engaged and plan their wedding, all of a sudden they push hard to look good. Suddenly, they regularly hit the gym, get a spray tan, even spend some serious moolah hiring a makeup artist, hairdresser, and a quality photographer. Why? Because they believe that these actions will make them look better on the big day. Then, once the wedding's over, they get off the wagon and go back to their fatty ways (hey, no judgment here—remember, I bought Spanx!).

The point is, what people *believe* can be influenced, which means *actions* can be influenced.

Translate this idea to sales volume, or essentially the growth and prosperity of your business. If your company isn't clearly and consistently stating what it believes in, there remains a high likelihood you'll be lost in the shuffle. If you tell the world what you believe and stand for it, however, you actually have a chance of influencing people and getting them to authentically love you.

> Hey McDonald's, you picking up what I'm laying down?

Of course, all of that said, you have to do the work.

For a moment, get real honest with yourself—how much time have you and your organization taken to codify your core beliefs and assess how they guide your actions? If you're like most of the world, hardly any.

I can't tell you how many companies I've worked with where I ask a group of people, "What does your company stand for—what's your core belief?" and if there are 15 people, I get 15 different answers. It's because most organizations and their leaders don't do the work to figure it out. I don't blame them. Look, it's challenging to dig into what you believe—but if you do, you open up so many amazing potential possibilities.

If you don't know what you stand for, how will you know what to tell the world? You'll act without knowing why. You'll make decisions like pulling cigarettes off the shelf for health reasons, while still stocking the shelves with booze, chips, and chocolate bars.

You won't know what to shout from the rooftops. And if you don't stand for something, how will your customers know who you truly are?

Short answer:

They won't. You'll be left in the dust, because you can't give them what you don't have.

CHAPTER 3

YOU CAN'T GIVE WHAT YOU DON'T HAVE

"Authentic brands don't emerge from marketing cubicles or advertising agencies. They emanate from everything the company does."

—HOWARD SCHULTZ

Quick! I need a $100 bill! Don't ask questions; just look in your wallet and see if you have one of those Ben Franklins lying around. Do you have one? Is it in your pocket?

If you find one, perfect—hand it over. If not, it doesn't matter how many times I ask for it, you can't give me a $100 bill if you don't have it. Sure, you could go to the ATM or ask your neighbors—maybe even cobble a hundred bucks together in small bills and loose change. But you can't give me what you don't have.

Now try this: I need your driver's license. I'll give it right back, I promise. But quick, just for the exercise, hand it over. Thank you. See, you could give that to me no problem because you had it on hand, right there in your wallet. But not the $100 bill. Why?

Because you can't give what you don't have.

Seems obvious, right?

Now look at it in light of your core belief: If you don't know your core belief, how will your customers—or worse, your potential customers—know it?

How can you give them something to latch onto if you don't have a core belief to give them?

If you don't know what you stand for, how will anyone else?

You'll recall the Carrot McMuffin from Chapter 1 (oh, what—you thought I'd zip past that monstrosity with little commentary?). Now why on Earth would McDonald's offer such a strange menu item? Because they don't have a single, clearly defined core belief. They've muddled their message by trying to appeal to everyone—so they appeal to no one.

In this chapter, I'll show you just how important it is to have a core belief to get customers to listen to you—without spending every Ben Franklin you have (or don't have).

DON'T YOU DARE PUT THOSE OREOS ON THE SHELF

Whole Foods' core belief, in highly paraphrased language, is: "Your body is a temple, and we offer only the cleanest, purest foods to support it." That's so deeply woven into their DNA that they can say no to stocking Oreos, Coca-Cola, and cigarettes without question. Then, as consumers—because Whole Foods acted in congruence with this core belief—we know it, too. We know that if we want organic, minimally processed, locally grown, ancient whole grains, Whole Foods is the place. But if you want a 96-pack of Diet Coke and a pallet full of Oreos, you go to Costco.

Even after Amazon purchased Whole Foods, they knew they weren't operating just another grocery store. They honored the core beliefs of the store and didn't put soda and Oreos on the shelves. If Amazon had, the loyal Whole Foods customers would have immediately left. It would add confusion—people wouldn't know where to go for their clean, hormone-free, grass-fed food.

It's like when Starbucks tried to sell wine (yes, it failed).

Or when McDonald's tried to sell pizza (seriously). Dig a little on YouTube and you'll find the original TV commercials for McPizza...it's brilliantly awful.

SPIRIT AIRLINES: THE BEST WORST AIRLINE IN THE WORLD

I love Spirit Airlines because they are unabashed about what they're about: They are *ridiculously* cheap. Thirsty, want water on the flight? You pay for it. You want to bring a travel essential, like luggage? Great, you've got to pay for that, even if it's carry-on. Enjoy boarding early? Awesome, you pay for it. Of course, they'll ask for the money with a smile on their face.

Every action they take is from the core belief that they are the cheapest airline going—end of story. Is it the most convenient? No. Are they the most comfortable? Absolutely not—they'll pack you in like a sardine on a chair seemingly void of padding.

But are they cheap? Hell. Yes. If your No. 1 criteria for picking a flight is cost, if you believe what Spirit believes, then your decision is nothing shy of obvious. In fact, they scream it out loud every opportunity they get.

I love Spirit for their commitment to their core belief, but good luck finding me on one of their flights. My beliefs look more like fancy lounges with free Wi-Fi, cheese cubes, and first-class upgrades. Yes, I'd love a glass of champagne before we take off. Cheers!

Having said all that, here are the most important words in this book so far:

It doesn't matter what your core belief is. What matters is actually having one, sticking to it, and shouting it proudly. People will flock to you. And that means the *right* people: the people who share that same belief.

EXCEPTION TO THE RULE: ULINE

Uline is an interesting company—their core belief is long, but mostly clear: "We believe good service means offering the finest quality and best selection of products with the quickest service in the industry. As long-term partners, we hope to exceed our customers' expectations—delivering every order with speed, passion, and operational excellence."

What do they do? In short, they handle all the stuff a warehouse would use to get their products to customers, like corrugated boxes, packing tape, pallet wrap, etc. They have a tremendous number of products, they're all high quality, and they have a huge staff of customer service reps to help you get them. They also have a robust website that's easy to navigate—it's all about customer service and making things easy for you.

What could be better? Everything they do resonates with me...almost.

If you dig *just* a bit deeper, you'll see what they stand for politically and socially: They seem to be anti-everything and everyone who isn't male, white, Christian, straight, and born in the United States. From my perspective, they value hate over love.

And there's the rub. As a customer, their core beliefs place me smack dab in the middle of a difficult crossroad: I love what they provide as a business partner, but vehemently disagree with the things they stand for personally.

This happens all the time. And it happens to you, too!

As much as I dislike what the owners may stand for, and after significant due diligence to find another company that could offer us the same products, I'm back to Uline. Nobody offers the same service, selection, and price. Against my better judgment, even though I don't believe in the owning family's beliefs, I still buy from them. I begrudgingly hit buy when I click that button on their website. Yes, companies can stand for something ugly and still succeed, because a better option simply doesn't exist.

I will give Uline one thing—they do a great job of telling people what they believe!

SUCCEEDING DESPITE YOURSELF

There are other companies that truly have no idea what they stand for and still succeed. One great example is UPS. By all standards and measures, they're a heck of a company—they get a lot right. We all know the eponymous brown trucks, and if I said, "What does Brown do for you?" you'd know I'm talking about UPS.

But let me ask you: What do they stand for?

Is it speed?

Reliability?

Customer service?

It's unclear. They've grown in the last decade because e-commerce companies like Amazon and Etsy have created a rising tide, which has lifted all boats, including UPS, DHL, and FedEx.

It's not that UPS offers anything exceptional, it's more that they have benefitted from larger trends.

Sometimes, a blind squirrel finds an acorn...

Don't be a blind squirrel.

COMMUNICATE IT OR KISS IT GOODBYE

If you're not, imagine for a moment that you're the CEO of a firm. Now, imagine again that you don't know what the company stands for. Let's start there.

OK Captain CEO, you institute a new initiative to boost sales. You order the HR department to actively search for a new head of sales, and you work alongside the CFO to develop comp plans for the entire sales team, as well as the CMO to develop a better message and main presentation deck. Got it? Awesome.

Now what happens? Crickets. Blank stare. Cut to black.

Every department you've ordered to do something is going to struggle.

The HR department, the marketing team, and the CFO are going to struggle because they have to know what you *believe* in order to take the next steps. The CFO needs to know what the firm values and how you think about employees to know how to best compensate them. The marketing team needs to know what you value in the products or services. To take appropriate action, they need to know what you and the company believe.

Just for fun, let's add another curveball to the example: You're an aggressive, Brooklyn-born CEO best described with a style that's loud, direct, and in-your-face. Simultaneously, the HR team thinks a softer, more empathetic style of leader is best. There are obvious contrasts here because of different beliefs, which stymies HR. Do they get a head of sales that appeases you? Eventually HR chooses to appease *themselves*, and goes with a gentle West Coast yoga guy who doesn't match your vision one bit.

All the while, you're pissed because you didn't get what you wanted—you wanted a white-collar version of legendary Chicago Bears head coach Mike Ditka, but instead you got a walking granola bar straight out of Whole Foods. It's a mess.

I see this happen all the time, and it's a damn shame. A new person will be hired and assigned a task, but the underlying belief of their role was never made clear—or maybe it was clear to some exec, but it was never communicated. Then, the new person comes in and starts changing things, and people start wondering just what the heck is going on here?

They don't know the right action to take because there is no core belief driving their role.

The point is, having a clear core belief you know deeply is fundamentally important. Think of it as a roadmap or blueprint. It gets customers to listen, it helps you engage with consistency inside the organization, and it helps you hire effectively.

Who knows, maybe your core belief could even save your life?

THE SS *ENDURANCE*

At its most basic level, any business will always be reliant on people. You have to get the right people, no matter what. Ernest Shackleton knew how to get the right people:

By standing for something and making his beliefs clear.

Shackleton was an intrepid explorer of the early 20th century, hunting for fame and fortune by exploring the uncharted corners of the Earth. In 1910, he set out on a journey to the South Magnetic Pole in his tall ship, the *Endurance.*

To find people he could trust on this journey, he put out a want ad: "MEN WANTED—for hazardous journey, small wages, bitter cold, long months of complete darkness, constant danger, safe return doubtful, honor and recognition in case of success."

He didn't sugarcoat what the experience would entail. There was no promise of a luxurious cruise with bikini-clad mermaids amid sun-kissed saltwater tide pools. No. Shackelton looked for and proceeded to find people with his same core beliefs by telling them exactly what they were getting into:

A dangerous expedition with incredibly high risks and equally high rewards.

Shackleton found his men and soon the entire team departed from New Zealand heading directly toward Antarctica. Not long after, their ship became trapped in an ever-growing sea of ice, where it stayed for more than a year. Can you imagine that? Stuck on a boat, surrounded by ice, somewhere between New Zealand and Antarctica for 12 whole months.

When it became clear the ice wasn't retreating, Shackleton ordered a small party to Australia to summon help for the crew and the *Endurance*, which was literally being crushed by ice.

In the meantime, put yourself on that boat for even a single hour. It's not like there was a Chick-fil-A just around the corner where the stranded crew could enjoy a delightful deep-fat-fried chicken filet sandwich. No, these guys were stuck in the middle of absolutely nothing. Remember, they only had the supplies they brought with them.

Eventually, against amazing odds, a rescue party returned to save the ship. Throughout this frozen, arduous journey, can you guess how many of the 28-person crew died?

Zero.

Ernest Shackleton found the right people for the job: those who shared the same core beliefs he did—those who could endure. And it made all the difference in the world.

You can always teach people skills. That's mostly easy. But you can't teach people what they believe. That has to be deeply rooted in who they are.

Simply put, you can't find those highly devoted

people—whether they're employees, customers, or advocates—unless you stand up and shout what you believe first, no matter how many Ben Franklins you try to give them.

PART II

IDENTIFYING CORE BELIEFS

CHAPTER 4

GETTING TO THE ROOT OF BELIEF

"If you tell me, it's an essay. If you show me, it's a story."

—BARBARA GREENE

He couldn't do it—he literally could not articulate his *why*.

I was standing in front of a whiteboard with an experienced, highly trained product sales manager named Mark and I kept asking him, "Why do you do what you do?"

He kept writing *what* he did (sell software) and *how* he did it (with special customer service), but he just wasn't getting to *why*.

It's funny: Mark's not unique in that sense. As business leaders, we're so wired to focus our attention and messaging on what we do and how we do it—and then if we still have a little time left, why we do it. But you know what? The truly great brands *start* with why, then they eventually answer how and what. In that precise order.

> You've watched the Simon Sinek TED video by now, so you know this already...right?
>
> Even if you have, it's difficult to make the shift from WHAT to WHY first. Very difficult.

When I speak in front of large groups, I like to put people similar to Mark on the spot. I know it's bad, and someday I'm probably going to get punched, but it's just too much fun! My audiences are full of senior leaders, founders, CEOs, senior vice presidents, etc., and most of them don't know how to answer *why* they do what they do.

Invariably, they say, "Money. I've got a family, which means bills to pay and mouths to feed."

I say, "Yeah, yeah, fine. Aaaaand you're wrong. That's an *outcome* of your effort, not why you do what you do. Keep digging."

From there, they get mad at me and struggle to answer—as Mark did—and don't come close to the true answer. Then I tell them (just like I told you for the second time and now the third time) to check out the third-most-watched TED Talk ever with Simon Sinek, where he outlines the Golden Circle.

It's the best way I know to get to the root of your beliefs.

THE GOLDEN CIRCLE EXERCISE

The Golden Circle is simple: You have three concentric circles. The smallest circle at the center says *why*, the next largest ring says *how*, and the biggest outer ring says *what*. The vast majority of companies communicate from the outside in—what, how, why—but the most successful companies start from the center out—why, how, what.

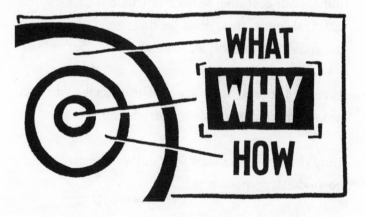

I looked at Mark and said, "Dude, it's a pretty simple model—why, how, what."

"Well, I'm a product manager for a little software tool that allows customers to have online chats with people like

BMW dealership operators. So I guess I'm Mark, and I believe deeply in actual conversations. What we've built is an online tool that allows you to converse directly with—"

"Whoa, Mark, dude, you're close! Just change the order."

"What do you mean?"

I said, "Try this: Hi, I'm Mark and I believe deeply in actual conversations. We do that by creating online tools that allow for real-time, one-on-one user experiences, where a human on a website can chat with another human, our customer service rep, to make a profound, real-deal connection. What we do is build the software that allows you to easily add that widget to your website."

He paused, looked at me like he'd just won the lotto, and said, "Holy crap, that was so much better."

"They're your words, Mark. All I did was precisely follow the model: why, how, what."

I've experienced this kind of transformation literally thousands of times now. The thing is, everyone thinks they're different, and every company thinks they're unique. Sorry, but we're all the same. You're no different—no better, no worse.

In the course of these exercises, I've been told things like this: "It doesn't matter if my hourly customer service reps know *why* we do what we do. I'm the CEO, and as long as I know, we're good."

Wrong. You're both equal human beings. If it matters why you do what you do, then it matters for everyone in your organization.

And look, there's a reason people don't do this. It takes years to uncover why and dig into this stuff. Plus it can be deeply emotional. It's hard! Most people aren't willing to work through that struggle.

Try the exercise yourself and see just how hard it is.

REGRET INSURANCE

The CEO of a $20 billion financial firm was crying so hard I could barely understand him.

"I've been doing it wrong all these years."

We'd just gone through the Golden Circle exercise. For thirty years on the job, he'd talked to customers about his company's retirement plans and how brilliantly designed the plan was relative to fiduciary regulations, and so on. But what he realized in that conversation with me was that he wasn't selling people a well-designed retirement plan.

He was selling peace of mind.

He was only now realizing it. He helped people retire with dignity, safety, security, and the peace of mind that when they stopped working they would actually be OK.

So it was emotional for him to see that *why*. He'd been leaving the humanity of his work behind for decades.

"I can't even imagine how easy it would have been to sell for all those years if I had just known what I know today."

If he had started with why, he could walk into a sales presentation saying, "I'm not here to sell you a 401(k). I'm here to sell you peace of mind. I believe, as does my firm, in comfort. What we want for you and your family is to feel safe and secure—comfortable no matter what. We'll do that by putting together amazing plans that check all the boxes of fiduciary management." If he had simply followed the Golden Circle, everything would have changed.

We all want to be connected to a purpose, and we all want meaning in our lives. We want to be part of the greater good. It's just a matter of articulating it. That's what this chapter will show you: how to reach the root of your core belief.

THE PROCESS OF DEDUCTION: FIND THE *WHY* FROM INSIDE THE JAR

"I do it for my family."

When people say that, it's always a lie—that's not exactly why anyone does anything. If all you wanted to do was provide for your family, you could do that working at Foot Locker. Or by selling illegal drugs to third graders, but you don't. (By the way, you better not be selling drugs to third graders!)

So, then, why exactly do you do what you do?

It's a tough question for individuals, and it's a tough question for organizations. They—or better stated as the people in charge of an organization—get flummoxed when you ask them directly what their core belief is. Most give some version of the typical vision and mission statement nonsense, but it's almost always a cop-out.

To get there, you'll need to guide yourself through a process of deductive reasoning. Yeah, you may have to hire an outside firm—it's often far easier to read the label from outside the jar—but with some focus and tenacity, you can still do it from inside the jar.

Here's the key: *Reverse engineer* your beliefs based on your actions.

WHAT IS REVERSE ENGINEERING?

Reverse engineering is a process used to uncover information. For example, during World War II, British and American forces noticed that the Germans had gasoline cans with an excellent design, vastly superior to their own. They had easy-to-carry handles and a more logical rectangular design, compared to the Allies' triangular design. The Allies reverse-engineered copies of the German gas cans, ultimately creating a version still in use today.

I know, this stuff is hard. But alas, good news! Reverse engineering your actions is fairly easy.

Shall we?

UNCOVER YOUR ACTIONS, UNCOVER YOUR BELIEFS

Start by considering your behaviors—the things you regularly do.

Grab a yellow legal pad and a pen. Now, start listing your actions. Seriously, just start thinking and writing. What do you do on a day-to-day basis?

Do you regularly send birthday greetings via LinkedIn? Maybe Facebook? Perhaps an email with a fun animated GIF? Wait, is it possible that you send an actual greeting card?

Do you hold a midday power nap sacred? You know, twenty-two minutes every day, at exactly 2:05 p.m., when you go to the nursing mothers' room, even though you're a man, to grab some power z's?

Do you knock back a daily protein-shake lunch, sitting at your desk, no matter how pasty and gritty they actually taste?

The list will be long, and from those scribbles, your job is to look for congruences and patterns. We routinely go through this process because we know full well that your beliefs rule your actions. So it stands to reason, if you can uncover your actions, you can eventually deduce your beliefs.

Again, I promise, this will eventually all make sense.

CONGRUENCE AND INCONGRUENCE

I am currently working with a healthcare firm boasting about 3,000 employees in India, and about 600 here in the US. They are killing it—in a good way, that is. Although they're successful now, there are significant incongruences between what they say and what they do. For example, their sales presentation deck is a bomb of what and how, with no core beliefs whatsoever.

But if you sit across the table from Abisheik, the CEO and founder, and ask him what his company is all about, he'll give you a great answer.

"We believe healthcare needs to change. It's too hard for the average person. The processes are inefficient, impractical, and confusing. And that the person suffering most as a result of this inefficiency is the one already suffering with their health problem. For us, that's wholly unacceptable."

That's a beautiful core belief. But their materials only

show a numbing phalanx of numbers and factoids: blah blah blah, what what what.

What Abisheik said and what he displayed were incongruent. It's equivalent to a self-proclaimed Chicago Bears fan dressing in green and gold and cheering for the Packers to win the Super Bowl. (That's also wholly unacceptable. And no actual Bears fan would ever stoop to something so low and despicable.)

It had never occurred to him that this incongruence existed—like most people, their company didn't *look*, they just did. So when they built a presentation deck for a pitch to Aetna or Blue Cross, it never crossed their mind to start with those well-crafted, meaningful core beliefs.

It works for most companies in the short term, but over time, those incongruences will lead to major breakdowns. All of a sudden, as firms like Abisheik's grow, what comes out of the CEO's mouth is one thing, but the people in the office three states away are creating their own narrative.

Once we pointed out these problems to him, he tightened up his control on the deployment of messaging before it was too late.

But for most firms, those incongruences lead you to getting the wrong clients—and even worse, the wrong people on your team. If you get the wrong people, it's because neither you nor your job candidates know what your firm believes.

WALT DISNEY: BACK TO THE FOUNDER

You know Disney people when you see them. They're chipper, squeaky clean, and obnoxiously happy. I have firsthand knowledge about this, because about a million years ago, I drove huge fiberglass submarines in the Magic Kingdom. Yeah, I'm one of them. To this day, people still take me for a Disney person because I just fit that mold. It seems like everywhere I go, just like my Disney days, a stranger gives me a cellphone to snap their picture or asks for directions.

But that wasn't always the case. I don't mean for me, but for Disney World at large.

When Disney World first opened in Orlando, it was built on a massive stretch of swampland where not much existed before. Within a few short years, the park opened to much fanfare, and quickly, the entire metro area expanded. This growth stressed the talent pool—there were only so many people to hire in central Florida, and eventually they ran out of candidates who fit the wholesome, bubbly personality that Disney was known for.

With demand rising, Disney found themselves hiring whomever they could find. This led to an incongruence for guests. The expectation was a magical, immersive experience presented by happy, delightful cast members. But when the talent pool ran dry, many guests experienced more mouse than Mickey. Visitors forked over big bucks for a promise that wasn't kept. Many vowed to never return, and you can be sure they told all their friends and family. The Disney brand was suffering.

The Disney team solved the issue by building on-site living quarters for seasonal employees in the form of bright, cheerful college kids from around the world. Rather than continuing to rely on their local geography, Disney intended to find people who believed what they believe and import the proper talent.

They chose people who fit the Disney ethos and instilled these new employees with the important lessons developed in the company from the very beginning. Whether you drive the boat on "The Jungle Cruise" or man the front desk at a resort hotel, during your first days of work, every new Disney employee takes a series of classes called *Traditions*. Here, you learn the origin stories of Walt and Roy Disney—how they were knocking on bankruptcy's door at least six times, and nothing but short instructional films for the US government during World War II kept them in business.

You can't go through something like that without knowing exactly what the company believes and stands for.

Disney went to their founders' stories to transmit—and through employees, shout—their core beliefs out loud. Today, they have not only emerged from those early struggles, but now the global entertainment juggernaut that is The Walt Disney Company consistently thrives.

From Pixar and Star Wars to ESPN and cruise ships, plus a myriad of magical theme parks around the globe, Disney believes in creating stories and experiences for the whole family. I predict they will continue to thrive, as long as they remember to teach every employee where it all came from.

INVESTIGATE FOUNDERS' STORIES

When every company started, it was for a reason. There was a problem to solve and a market opportunity. Regardless of your job title, I encourage everyone to discover as much information as you can about your company's beginnings.

Talk to the founders if they're still alive. You will learn a ton.

With every founder, you'll hear the little inflection or tipping points in the genesis of the company that made them think, "We need to do this." Look for those little flickers as that story eventually turns into the blaze that is your company's purpose.

JUNTO INSTITUTE: BEN FRANKLIN'S VISION

Benjamin Franklin gathered a group of business owners and other intellectuals, all interested in being better, gaining additional skills, and enjoying meaningful conversations. He called this gathering the Junto.

A couple hundred years later—from that inspiration— Raman Chadha, a professor of entrepreneurship at DePaul University in Chicago, founded the Junto Institute. He saw that the traditional MBA was only good enough. Raman felt MBA programs turned graduates into robotic, textbook-driven leaders who lacked emotional intelligence. As a result, sure, many people with MBAs were exposed to meaningful case studies, but they weren't good leaders.

He was also bothered by the fact that he taught entrepreneurship, but he wasn't an entrepreneur...he was a professor.

So Raman got to work. He diligently curated a large community of instructors and mentors, and created an immersive program for post-revenue company leaders who wanted to be more emotionally intelligent, better humans with better relationships in the office and at home. Something an MBA was not teaching them.

His core belief was that if we can make leaders more emotionally intelligent, it will make a huge and direct impact on their businesses. From that core belief, he created a truly loving and trusting environment, where people confided in each other, and they shared the ugly truth with each other.

As you might expect, the people and businesses who participated in the Junto Institute all experienced amazing growth in their company and in their relationships.

This unique kind of growth would never happen in an MBA class, and it's completely dictated by Raman's original belief about what makes a good leader. Look through your own company's story to figure out your core beliefs, as Raman did when he found Ben Franklin's story.

ARCHETYPES: YOUR BRANDING SHORTCUT

If your founders' stories aren't helping you find your core beliefs, archetypes are one of the coolest tools for zeroing in on your brand and marketing. You can hold archetypes up like a paint chip to give you one word, image, or persona that provides clarity around your elusive core beliefs.

You can read more about archetypes in lots of places, my favorite is archetypesinbranding.com, but in short, they are different types of characteristics that you may fit the mold of. These archetypes, such as the hero or villain, exist whether we know about them or not.

Look at me. I wear perfectly pressed, professionally laundered shirts, and I drive a hybrid. Never in a million years would you see me in a leather jacket riding a Harley. As such, I wouldn't have categorized myself as a maverick or rebel. If you look at the rebel archetype, however, you see that they break laws.

Well, I break every corporate "rule" I can. I make waves! I have no desire to do things like everybody else—I'm a nonconformist. Now, for the record, I'm not a counter-culture hippie or a drug-abusing, lawless troublemaker either, but I'm still very much a maverick and rebel.

Every day, we work on client projects where we create amazing things out of what seems to be thin air. From crafting powerful messages to designing visuals that knock your socks off, we're constantly pulling rabbits from hats. Another big archetype for my brand: magician.

Recognizing these archetypes helped me zero in on our core branding—the things we believe in and stand for.

Your archetype won't necessarily tell you your core beliefs, but recognizing your archetype for yourself or your company might provide the necessary scaffolding you need to chisel away at a core belief that is already there. It's hard to pull this stuff out of thin air, and archetypes are a spectacular cheat sheet.

Through this process of finding your archetype (or archetypes—we're often a unique blend of a few), you will illuminate and put words to feelings that you've always felt or known but can't quite articulate, and that's just straight-up cool.

You may even reverse engineer your core beliefs based on your archetype and find that they are actually completely outlandish—and that's liberating!

Once it's clear, you can go out and live it authentically. The companies that discover those core beliefs and truly embrace them almost always have great brands.

WHAT WOULD NO. 2 DO?

If I asked you, "What is the single largest car rental company—by both revenue and transaction volume?" what would your answer be?

The answer is Hertz, by a big margin. As such, Avis has long embraced the tagline: "We're No. 2, so we try harder."

Don't you just love that? That's their way of saying that they realize that Hertz enjoys more locations, more counter space, more cars, and more employees. So Avis will stand out to the customer base by not going for price, not going for most convenient locations, and not hiring more employees. They can't compete on those factors.

They will focus on customer service, a bigger smile, a cleaner car, faster in-and-out time, and a better overall experience. They've positioned themselves as underdogs, and they own that archetype.

For example, from my rebel and magician archetypes,

I found our core belief: we make waves. I've made that pretty clear in this book, and we make that remarkably clear at SquarePlanet in general. We're upfront about that in all we do. We're going to cause some trouble. Of course, what that really means is this: We're not simply going to tell you what you want to hear. We're going to provide you the honest (and sometimes ugly) truth.

One of my favorite clients is a charming guy named Pete. He is responsible for literally billions of dollars in his work with one of the largest entities in healthcare. If you've been to a hospital, there is a decent chance Pete had a hand in your treatment, but not the way doctors and nurses do. It's a twisted tale, but it's all about supply chain, or the "stuff" used at a hospital. Beyond his natural charisma, Pete is quick, smart, funny, and very creative. His ideas are usually gold.

Picture this: We're putting the final touches on a huge meeting; Pete is onstage, rehearsing his keynote presentation for his firm's largest annual event and he wants a very specific kind of teleprompter.

As the guy in charge, and with all the grace of a tranquilized three-legged antelope, I say, "Well Pete, you're not getting one."

He was shocked and completely bent out of shape with

blueprint. It gets customers to listen, it helps you engage with consistency inside the organization, and it helps you hire effectively.

Who knows, maybe your core belief could even save your life?

THE SS *ENDURANCE*

At its most basic level, any business will always be reliant on people. You have to get the right people, no matter what. Ernest Shackleton knew how to get the right people:

By standing for something and making his beliefs clear.

Shackleton was an intrepid explorer of the early 20th century, hunting for fame and fortune by exploring the uncharted corners of the Earth. In 1910, he set out on a journey to the South Magnetic Pole in his tall ship, the *Endurance*.

To find people he could trust on this journey, he put out a want ad: "MEN WANTED—for hazardous journey, small wages, bitter cold, long months of complete darkness, constant danger, safe return doubtful, honor and recognition in case of success."

All the while, you're pissed because you didn't get what you wanted—you wanted a white-collar version of legendary Chicago Bears head coach Mike Ditka, but instead you got a walking granola bar straight out of Whole Foods. It's a mess.

I see this happen all the time, and it's a damn shame. A new person will be hired and assigned a task, but the underlying belief of their role was never made clear—or maybe it was clear to some exec, but it was never communicated. Then, the new person comes in and starts changing things, and people start wondering just what the heck is going on here?

They don't know the right action to take because there is no core belief driving their role.

The point is, having a clear core belief you know deeply is fundamentally important. Think of it as a roadmap or

They sent me so much information that I thought we'd need a larger Dropbox account. PowerPoint decks, online resources, in-person meetings at their Phoenix facility—we even did video interviews at their Nashville office. We did copious amounts of due diligence and got all the information we could.

I even asked for personal stories from Tony and found a doozy.

NEVER FAIL TO HELP AGAIN

Tony was in an airline lounge. It was one of those smaller satellite lounges and it was jam-packed. The only seat he could find was directly next to the buffet lines of finger food. He had settled in, computer open, and he was focused on maintaining his working space.

He looked up and saw an older gentleman around his father's age, struggling with luggage while trying to carry a plate of food. Tony realized that the lost-looking older man didn't have a seat, was overmatched by the heavy bags, and his precarious plate of food was soon to be the straw that broke the camel's back.

Tony saw what was about to happen from a mile away—within two steps, the man dropped his plate of airport lounge nibbles all over the floor.

Before it happened, Tony accurately summarized the situation, but failed to prevent it. No doubt about it, he could have helped.

But he was comfy. He'd finally settled into his nest of a seat, and he's a very busy guy. Running a global firm with 18,000 associates isn't a walk in the park. He simply didn't have time to break his own rhythm and flow.

Almost immediately, Tony got mad—not at the old man, but at *himself.* He stood up—now too late to stop the drop, but still able to assist.

"Sir, I got it. You go find a seat. I'll get a customer service rep—don't worry about all of this."

The old man was more embarrassed than anything else, but thankful for Tony's help. The thing was, as Tony cleaned the floor, he was furious with himself. He could have helped this man *before he dropped everything.*

He thought of Asurion. He realized that as an organization, they would never fail to be actually helpful, just like he'd failed in that moment.

He said his core belief is to be helpful, but if he sits there and doesn't help, he's a fraud. This is real to Tony. This experience hit him hard, and so will the experience you have that helps you recognize your core beliefs.

Striving from that core, Asurion employees can look back and say they made a lot of money and built a business that gave people jobs, but they can also say that along the way, they made life better for people because they were actually truly helpful. It's bigger than profit and loss statements and balance sheets and bottom lines. It's real life, and that's the stuff that matters.

Tony has demonstrated the courage necessary to move beyond generic beliefs on a poster and move into something deeply meaningful. The generic beliefs weren't wrong or bad, they're just benign. Completely vanilla. It takes a true leader to move away from the safety of vanilla, because you *will* alienate people. But your goal is to only work with people who believe what you believe.

It's incredibly hard to say to the 18,000 associates at Asurion, "Hey, the reason we exist—the thing we stand for—is to be actually helpful. If you don't believe that, go look for a new job." It's easier to do nothing. It takes substantial courage to change. Tony was willing to do that.

BADTESTING: THE MAN WHO COULD SEE THE MATRIX

My client—his name is Shachar, but everyone simply calls

him Shak—is a crazy-smart guy with a brilliantly named company: BadTesting. The idea is pretty simple: They do quality assurance on websites and other software products before they go live.

Every time I think of Shak, I think of *The Matrix*. Yeah, Shak may not have the physique, and he's usually in jeans and a T-shirt, but he's just like Neo. Here's what I mean: There's the famous scene near the end of *The Matrix* when you see the world through Neo's eyes, with the green symbols dripping down on the black background—the Matrix itself. That's Shak's vision when he looks at websites.

He can open up a website the same way you or I would, then he looks into the code and says, "Oh, there's a problem here. Oh, and another one there. We'll have to fix those."

I watched him work on a casino website once and it was an impressive masterclass, even though I know nothing about coding. He was looking at the code for the age input field as the user opens the site.

"What's wrong with that?" I said. "That's just where you put a date, isn't it?"

"Well, no, because if you go down here..." he scrolled

down 18 pages of code, "you'll see that if you don't enter it in the exact right way, it will cause a problem here."

He pointed to a specific line of code and looked at me like I would understand. I was blown away. He had this mental model of what the site's code looked like, and he knew exactly what it had to be. He could read the matrix. He was playing 9D chess, while the people who built the site were playing checkers.

It's amazing. He's practiced his craft at a high level for huge clients for a long time. But even so, he was never really able to explain what it was he did, how it worked, or why it matters to him or his clients. He just kind of went along, operating.

He is a for-real nice guy, super interesting, and a bit socially awkward, but I've enjoyed every interaction I've ever had with him. And it was clear from the outset that he is a genius. He fit the savant archetype 100 percent.

Again, when I worked with him, I asked him to hand over all of his materials—but unlike other clients, he didn't have a lot of stuff to sift through. He hadn't written much copy, and he didn't have a lot of employees we could interview. It was just Shak doing his thing.

I had to look at his actions and reverse engineer his core

beliefs from there. I hung out with him, had him show me exactly what he does, and how he does it. I discovered that like Neo in *The Matrix*, he could see what others couldn't. After recognizing that, he used that angle as part of his marketing platform: "No matter how small a mistake is, it's still a mistake. Let me fix it for you before you go live."

He was eventually able to grow his client roster, speak at industry events, and build out his own website—simply because he was able to put into words what he couldn't articulate before.

TOWEL MANAGEMENT

No doubt about it, my favorite person on the planet is my wife, Shawna. She's remarkable. Of course, everyone who knows us constantly reminds me of that. I'm incredibly lucky to have her as my partner in life, and, seriously, she's the best thing that's ever happened to me.

Contrary to what you hear from many couples, we both say our marriage has been easy. Except for one thing—towel management.

See, when Shawna gets out of the shower and dries herself off and puts on her robe, she quickly wraps her towel around her head. No problem there, pretty standard operating procedure. Eventually, it's time to blow dry her hair. That's when she would do the unthinkable—she threw her towel *wherever* she wanted! I'd find them on the back of the sofa, on the kitchen countertop, on the freshly made bed—everywhere. Once, I found her towel in the garage. How is that even possible?

That damp towel would lay there for God knows how long.

Eventually, it became a joke: "Hey babe, I'm looking for the toaster, do you know if it's hanging on your towel rack?" We'd laugh because she was truly unaware that she was even doing it.

What was so obvious to me was completely invisible to her, and it serves as a brilliant illustration: It's hard to read the label from *inside* the jar. It's a simple action, hanging up a towel, but Shawna could rarely do it without me pointing out where she missed the mark.

It's a parallel many companies face when they start to zero in on their core beliefs: How do you get to the root of your core beliefs without some outside counsel? It's tough, but these lessons will help you do it better.

If you fill out the Golden Circle—why, how, what—if you focus on all *whats*, you're in trouble. Sure, this is the fate of most organizations and the people who occupy them.

But you're not getting to the root—the core belief. When you do this, when you stand for something, there is a far-greater likelihood you'll build a brand people authentically love.

Every now and then, I'm faced with a scenario that I actually relish. Sometimes an organization, usually a small or brand-new one, can't find a core belief. They just aren't there. Sometimes it's a bigger organization, even a fully developed one, but the leadership team or owner isn't "wired" for this kind of stuff.

No worries! You can aspire to be more than what you are. You can aspire to, say, put the towel on the rack.

Your core belief may be incomplete. That's totally fine. In the next chapter, I'll show you how to craft aspirational core beliefs that are distinctive and contour your organization's actions toward your *intended* direction—if not your current direction—to get your customers to listen and act.

CHAPTER 5

ASPIRATIONAL BELIEFS

"If you can dream it, you can do it."

—WALT DISNEY

Nikola Motor Company builds vehicles that run on hydrogen power.

They also have this very small, little, minor desire: to completely, fundamentally change transportation as we know it. You know, no biggie. From that one central premise, or basis of a core belief, they have engineered and built the most cutting-edge, tech-heavy semi-truck ever. It runs on hydrogen power, its only emission is pure water, and it can go up steep mountain grades at 60 mph.

Oh, they also built a personal watercraft (think Jet Ski), and a stealthy, military-grade off-road 4x4 with room for a big gun and a drone. Plus another hydrogen-powered truck specifically for use in the narrow, twisted routes of Europe.

Again, just some minor, basic stuff here...you know, just another typical start-up.

If your core beliefs are impossible to nail down, it's absolutely conceivable that you can strive for something greater than what you already are. The aspiration has to be well within the framework of realistic possibilities. That's what Nikola has done.

They have a bold, imaginative leader who built and later sold technology businesses. They have engineers, designers, and a slew of dedicated people eager to change the face of transportation. They don't have a manufacturing facility nor the skilled employee base to build them. At this point, however, they've sold 800 trucks to Anheuser-Busch, based on a prototype and a dream. Now that's something!

Nikola is only a startup—a billion-dollar one, but a startup nevertheless—yet they've still managed to say, "Let's rally around a single, powerful core belief and move from there."

Aspirational core beliefs can be game-changers, but they have to be within the realm of realistic possibility. For

Nikola, creating these amazing new vehicles is more than just possible—it's actually happening.

If done correctly, they are as good as any tool in your business to change the world, even if you don't make world-changing vehicles.

THE PUBLIC CAN SNIFF OUT BULLSHIT

The public can tell when your aspirational core beliefs are too far outside your realm of expertise.

I hate to pick on them, but they make it so easy: Look at McDonald's. They promised they'd switch to all cage-free eggs in their syrupy, sugar-soaked breakfast sandwiches. Great. Do they really believe in health food? Probably not, but we'll let that slide.

When they made that announcement, people did the math and realized there weren't enough cage-free eggs available in the *entire country* to account for their egg consumption alone. Now what? Everyone looks at their claim and says, "Come on." They have no legs to stand on, and it makes them look worse than if they'd just kept their mouths shut in the first place. They aspired to an unrealistic core belief and it cost them more PR headaches they could have avoided.

HOW TO CRAFT ASPIRATIONAL CORE BELIEFS

You heard it with Nikola, and I'll say it again: there has to be a kernel of truth to your aspirational core belief.

Do yourself a favor and sift through every outward-facing,

company-centric element in your arsenal. Website, marketing brochure, explainer video on YouTube, core presentation deck, business cards, social media pages, email signature line—the list goes on and on.

Review these materials, do a deep dive and be completely honest, assessing what works in your company right now and extrapolate where it could be used in the future.

I'm doing this exact work with a client out of Lincoln, Nebraska, called Ameritas. This century-old firm sells insurance and other financial products, like 401(k)s. More than anything else, Ameritas believes in customer service.

They believe in speaking to people when they call, even finding answers to their questions. Amazing! The crazy part? Their technology is fairly antiquated. I mean, I half expected to walk in there and see one of those old, gigantic IBM computers with the black screens and green text. OK, it's way better than that, but cutting edge? Not so much.

There are plenty of firms in the industry with far-better technological resources, but their core beliefs have nothing to do with customer service. They have app-based user interfaces where you may be able to review your portfolio while sitting at a baseball game, but best of luck if you have a question that needs answering in mere moments.

Not Ameritas. They care most about customer service—it's why they exist. They believe the financial journey should be something you don't have to struggle with. They never want you to feel like you're all alone, trying to manage the mostly unmanageable.

The thing is, Ameritas hasn't been around for more than 100 years by sitting still—they *get it*. They know we like having that app to check out our portfolio during the ballgame. They know competitors will try to win work by highlighting this weakness. So, while they work to integrate more technology into their operations, they lean into their core beliefs. Imagine a sales call from an Ameritas rep. You'd likely hear this: "We believe the technology you desire is on the way. We don't have it yet, but we will have a robust app, a website that's simple to navigate, and an easy way for you to get online and handle your retirement account in the ways you need. And in the meantime, you can always count on our world-class customer service to help you out."

It works because it's real and they're actively pursuing it. If they said they care about customer service and want tech to be part of that equation, but then have no backend development working behind the scenes, they'd just be liars.

Remember: if there's no kernel of truth behind an aspirational core belief, the processes you build out of it won't work.

Authenticity is fundamental to a core belief.

PUT YOUR STAMP ON IT—IF YOU HAVE SOMETHING TO SHIP

As a leader, it's easy to succumb to the desire to "put your stamp" on an organization. We've all seen it happen before: An organization changes its leadership—even in small companies, even within a department—and the new leader wants to change everything.

In many ways, that's a good development—but in other ways, it's troubling for those who were around before the new leader. Because in general, people are resistant to change.

In that circumstance, if you're the new leader or you've brought the new leadership in, a simple question can go a long way to making sure their "stamp" as a leader is a good one:

Simply ask the leadership team what they believe...what they stand for.

Here's a great example...

Transamerica is another retirement company. For a long time, they were all about education. They had a core belief that the more you know about retirement, the more money you'd try to save.

It worked for them. The more people knew about the power of their 401(k), the more money they'd pump into it, and the more Transamerica got as a spiff in the process. It was a win-win situation.

Their goal was education, education, and education. Their respected, likable leader even wrote a book called *Transform Tomorrow*, which was all about the importance of retirement funding.

Then he got the boot.

The new team simply didn't care about education. They cared about cutting costs, streamlining the business, and profits, profits, profits. All of a sudden, the people who had operated from the core belief that retirement education was good for their business felt isolated. They felt let down, even betrayed. In essence, the new leaders said, "We're all about maximizing profits. I don't want to spend time or incur costs on educational seminars or a book tour. Just go sell some shit."

It changed everything.

It killed morale. The best people left for greener pastures and the sales numbers in this division nose-dived.

But imagine if the succession was reversed—imagine if the first Transamerica leader was all about profits, but the second leader was all about education? He could come in and say, "Our aspirational core belief is that the whole country should know about retirement planning. So, we'll do that by educating everybody." Now that belief becomes something people can aspire to be and rally around. It can make things better, rather than getting worse.

In case you're wondering, we ditched our Transamerica 401(k) and decided to go with Ameritas. I told you beliefs lead to actions.

SIMPLICITY REIGNS SUPREME

"Never invest in a business you cannot understand."

—WARREN BUFFETT

Warren Buffett has provided a lot of wisdom to a lot of people over the years. One thing he has always postulated is: Don't invest in a business you can't understand. Successful companies, regardless of how complex their operations—such as a semi-autonomous electric car company—will have beliefs that you can explain simply. The companies he invests in are no different:

He owns Geico, which is an insurance company.

Buffett is the largest shareholder of Coca-Cola, a soft drink company.

And he owns Dairy Queen, a hamburger and ice cream chain.

Each of these is an easy-to-understand business. In theory, this is pretty straightforward. In practice? Another situation entirely. Put it this way: Do you really think Coca-Cola and its global distribution network is an "easy" business? How about the mountains of red tape in the insurance business? And delicious soft-serve ice cream is tasty, but could you begin to make, store, and serve it to hundreds of customers every day?

The idea with finding your core belief is the same. If the beliefs extolled by a senior leader, for example, are too large and complex, they'll never be adopted.

Your core beliefs can't be twenty-five things—but they can be two things.

Pharmaceutical companies, for example, could make incredibly detailed, scientifically engineered compounds made of molecules that create unique effects in the human body. Just look at chemotherapy to treat cancer. That's wildly complex science! But the core belief of the company could be something simple. It might be a small notion: "We exist to help people heal."

That's a simple notion, and valuable, even though the *whats* and *hows* of their business are incredibly complex.

So yes, Warren Buffett is right: simplicity reigns supreme. I'm not going to tell him he's wrong.

Will you?

No matter how complex your company is, it's no excuse to have an overly complicated core belief.

ARTIFICIAL COMPLEXITY

Unfortunately, in corporate communications, people feel the need to add complexity for no apparent reason.

I admonish my clients for this behavior. I say things like, "Don't give me that nonsense. I don't want the brochure answer. Enough with the corporate speak. Tell me for real what's actually going on here."

Them: "You know, to create a customer journey, the digital transformation begins with understanding intrinsic market psychographics and analytics all scrubbed through our proprietary algorithm using a..."

Me: "Stop. First, I just threw up in my mouth a little. Second, I'm a little offended that you're speaking such nonsense to me. I'm a human being. I'm not a laser printer you're sending instructional code to. Talk to me like a human. If it's not simple, people can't adopt it. If it's complex, people can't remember it. If it's jargon-filled, people won't believe it. It's gotta be human. It's gotta be simple."

I was working with an international client—a large grocery company—and the CEO was talking about their mission, but he couldn't quite articulate it.

He said, "You know what? Let me grab something real quick. I'll be right back."

He came back with a large sign that had been in the lobby and proceeded to read it to me. It was the formal, complete version of their corporate mission.

He finished and looked at me expectantly.

I said, "I think I know the issue. You're the fucking CEO. If you can't remember it, how can you expect a grocery-store cashier to know it?"

Far too often, companies' core beliefs are written by a committee or a group of people who think they'll get a gold star for sounding smart and corporate, but they're just making things artificially complex.

If the front line of your company can't remember your core belief and live it in their everyday lives, then it doesn't matter. It's no different than if it didn't exist at all.

He realized immediately that the name was misleading. The new CEO of Siteworx, Andrew Walker, just didn't like the name. He knew intrinsically that potential customers would limit their own thinking around the firm's core capabilities. They make a living by helping organizations build great websites, of course, but they do a lot of other things, too.

For one, they build custom software solutions that specifically address their customers' biggest pain points. By definition, that means they are all about partnerships— these guys live for amazing relationships with their clients. That's at the heart of everything they do. Siteworx as both a brand and a name felt more dated and narrower than their true aspiration.

Andrew, very aware of the massive expense, effort, and time to do so, decided to rebrand the firm to something that fit his aspirational vision of what the company *could* become in the future, as opposed to what it *has been* for a decade.

Some outside help was brought in, and eventually he chose a new name for the company: Shift7 Digital. Why Shift7 Digital? Because if you hit shift and the 7 key on a keyboard, it creates an ampersand: &. The whole point was that it takes two. Like peanut butter & jelly, client &

vendor—the ampersand spoke to the core idea that everything they did was based on two parties coming together. You know, a relationship.

Technology changes all the time. Constant evolution that we—both as users and consumers—are forced to manage. But through all that change, Andrew believed something could be more everlasting: relationships. He decided that a new name was the perfect vehicle for a new core belief that relationships matter most.

Simple, aspirational, and true. It's a great core belief.

Plus, it stands the test of time. Yesterday, they built websites. Today, they might build mobile apps for companies. Tomorrow, they might focus on cloud-based technology.

In ten years, Shift7 might work on automated vehicles. Whatever form it takes, it's known that the technology will constantly change, but their focus on relationships won't. Guided by that core belief, they focused on engineering delight for their clients.

The key here is that Andrew and his team are authentically great people. He imported trusted talent that he knew fit this mold. All of them care deeply about relationships—this isn't marketing hocus-pocus. It's real, and it's aspirational. So like ducks to water, people adopted it.

See, it has to be authentic. Even if your aspirational belief is not fully part of the structure of your organization, it can be over time.

The dedication to the core belief "relationships matter most" manifested in some easy ways, like giving both associates and customers really nice branded shirts and coffee mugs. But the coolest is what they did to redesign their offices.

While still a work in progress, Andrew directed his teams to create an "office within the office" for visiting clients. He picked the best spot within each of their offices around the country, tricked out the décor and furniture, and even added personal coffee makers. The idea is brilliant in its simplicity: Want a client to feel comfortable? Well, then provide them your most comfortable spot.

Even if clients don't use it, imagine a prospect coming in for a tour. How do you think they'd feel knowing that Andrew and his team value the relationship above all else? Remember, beliefs lead to actions. If the prospect also believes that relationships matter most and that technology is constantly changing, then Shift7 is going to get the work.

Siteworx was focused on building websites. Great. You can get that anywhere. Underwhelmed.

Shift7 focuses on building *relationships*.

Nothing Andrew did to align the company to their core beliefs was incredibly complex. Yes, they did have to spend real money on those changes, but it's not difficult. What was difficult was finding it—reverse engineering what they already did to get to their core belief.

CEO JEFF: A FORCE OF NATURE

My buddy Jeff has always been an opinionated loud-mouth—he'd be the first to admit that.

Some people are offended by him. Some people love him. He's not for everyone—he can drive you crazy. But don't let the above words fool you; Jeff is one of the people I respect, trust, and love most on the planet. If I needed help at 4 a.m. on a Tuesday in the dead of winter, Jeff is the first person I'd call.

Jeff started a company in a very competitive, price-sensitive space. His firm sells industrial supplies—if you need 16 different kinds of threaded bolts, four heavy-grit grinding discs, an eight-foot ladder, and three cases of duct tape, he's got you covered.

Under his leadership, the company, Fort Dearborn, achieved growth by brute force. Jeff is relentless—nobody outworks him. And nothing has been handed to him, either. Through thick and thin, Jeff has managed to create a wildly successful enterprise.

He's fueled expansion by buying up competitors, and he's integrated new people and added new facilities. A couple years ago, Fort Dearborn got to the point where it became a public-facing entity. Jeff needed a retail showroom, like a hardware store.

At that point, he came to me and said, "Come see this; I need your help."

I've known Jeff since my first week of college. We lived in the same dorm, became members of the same fraternity, were neighbors in Chicago for more than a decade, went to each other's weddings, etc. I *know* this guy.

We dug into his sales materials, looked around the retail store, asked him a bunch of leading questions, and pretty quickly realized he is the textbook definition of the "savior" archetype. While Jeff wears the savior role extremely well, it had never occurred to him before. It was obvious to me, yet a complete mystery to him—he saves the day.

That's why he would bail me out of a New Orleans jail during Mardi Gras, and that's why if you're a manufacturer and you need a very specific part, you could call Jeff and he'd have it to you in an hour.

If that meant he had to get on a space shuttle and have the part flown in from Mars, he'd do it.

Of course, Jeff had never seen it this way—he just worked. We could see that it was a very specific archetype, and we could wrap his savior tendencies into an aspirational core belief.

A perfect example of Jeff's heroism: He had a client who used a high volume of unique plastic trays. They had to be thoroughly washed after every use, and it was costing them a lot of money.

Jeff caught wind of this and pressed for more details. The client told him how much they spent on the cleaning service. They said the process was unreliable, expensive, and basically the worst part of what they do.

Jeff told them he could do it better—not a little better, *a lot* better. From scratch, the Fort Dearborn team literally built a carwash-like process for these trays in the back storeroom of one of his buildings. He hired a team of workers, made it a priority that these trays got done no matter what, and in every way, vastly improved the situation for his client.

But Jeff didn't look at it as a way to make money, or even as a way to save them money. That was just a happy byproduct of his actions. He just wanted to know their biggest problem and figure out a way to solve it.

And that was it. We helped him rebrand everything, even reframing their conversations.

Instead of asking their clients, "What part do you need?" or "What kind of grinding discs are you burning through?" we framed the question as...

"What's your biggest problem and how can Fort Dearborn solve it?"

That's a completely different aspiration than, "What part can I get you?"

He had never once thought of himself, his firm, or his actions as that of a hero, but that's exactly who he is, and that's exactly what they've been doing all along.

The industry is niche enough that Jeff's clients understand the nature of his query. "What's your biggest challenge and how can I solve it for you?" doesn't mean Jeff will find their next CEO or book a vacation house in Thailand for them. It means Jeff will get them the parts they need, solve a warehouse issue, or keep the manufacturing line running.

On the surface, it might appear that Jeff is bombastic and troublesome. Really, it's just his way of saying "I got you." Review your actions and your archetypes to help reveal what you truly believe. It may surprise you and those around you!

WHAT WOULD WALT DO?

Walt Disney has been dead since the late 1960s—my entire lifetime. And yet, the phrase "What Would Walt Do?" was still a huge part of that company's culture, even when I worked there in the summer of 2000.

It would be easy to say, "Let's just go for the dollars and make movies full of violence, nudity, and foul language," but that's not very Disney-like, is it?

He's not even alive and his presence still creates an aspiration that permeates the company and guides people's actions. Sometimes leaders are so visionary and so powerful that they leave an indelible mark—a shadow that casts long after they're dead.

Is that the type of legacy you want? Or would you rather add another zero to the bottom line?

Don't ask what I can do, or what Walt can do.

The question is: What can *you* do?

Will people be asking what you would have done in their shoes, decades after you're gone? Or will they be happy you're not there anymore?

CHAPTER 6

MISSING THE MARK

"It's the job of any business owner to be clear about the company's nonnegotiable core values. They're the riverbanks that help guide us as we refine and improve on performance and excellence. A lack of riverbanks creates estuaries and cloudy waters that are confusing to navigate. I want a crystal-clear, swiftly-flowing stream."

—DANNY MEYER

What do Liberia, Myanmar, and the United States share in common?

At first blush, it would seem not much. One is a little African nation, the other is a sky-high Himalayan country, and then you have the big bad United States. What could these three countries possibly have in common?

Here's the answer:

These are the only countries on the planet that don't regularly use the metric system.

Everyone else uses the base 10 metric system, which is easy and makes sense (I mean, zero degrees is freezing, and 100 degrees is boiling. That only seems logical). In the mid-1970s, Congress passed a law that mandated the metric system be taught in public schools. How did that work out?

Just look at a ruler, a thermometer, or speed limit sign. From an international perspective, we totally miss the mark, but nobody steps back to question why we use the outdated and inconvenient imperial system.

Far too many people and organizations never step back to question anything. They just *do*.

Are you just doing?

WHY? BECAUSE WE ALWAYS HAVE

I ask people all the time: "Why are you having this meeting?"

Too many of them answer, "Well, because we always have."

That's not how you teach and inspire people—by having unnecessary mandatory meetings. You do it by tapping into their emotive side, and articulating why you do the work you do.

But what happens when you don't want to articulate that why?

This is deep work that can, frankly, be quite uncomfortable. What if the people in your organization resist identifying core beliefs?

What if you identify it, but it misses the mark, so people find committing to it frightening, or they just don't want to change?

That's what we'll cover in this chapter.

WHY DO PEOPLE IGNORE OR RESIST CORE BELIEFS?

I've said it before, so I'll say it again: articulating *why* is deep work. People and organizations lack the awareness about why they exist, and instead focus only on what and how. Why do they do this?

Lots of reasons, but one is simply because it's easier.

Another reason to resist implementing strategies that lead with core beliefs is probably going to surprise you.

From a results standpoint, your core belief won't work. At least at first.

It probably won't drive sales, increase productivity, or get the right associates in your company in, say, the first month. It takes time. But if you align with those core beliefs, you will see those changes *over time.*

For most, it's easier to dance with what you already know and not change for fear of alienating customers. It's easier to say there are bigger fish to fry—more important things to pursue—than identifying your core beliefs.

I assure you: I've done a lot of metaphorical fishing in my day, and this is the biggest fish of all of them.

McDonald's should be focused on alienating customers—eventually serving far fewer people, but people who believe what they believe. Just imagine what *that* boardroom discussion would be like. If execs at their offices said they wanted to roll out a plan that would alienate a huge chunk of the population—they'd be murdered! They'd be accused of not serving the bottom line.

I know it's hard, but you have to let go of the notion that alienating people is a bad thing. You *will* alienate people, and that's a good thing. You want to work alongside those who share your core beliefs. As soon as you get warm and cozy with that foreign notion, all of this gets a lot easier.

PENSIONMARK: THE MOST EXPERIENCED PILOTS IN THE FINANCIAL INDUSTRY

It's hard to adopt this stuff, even when you have it nailed—just ask Pensionmark, a financial advisory firm. Based in Santa Barbara, California, this is a solid company of people making a real name for themselves in a crowded field.

In fact, they have an older, highly experienced, very stable team of financial advisors. Their average tenure is much older than practically any other firm out there.

Pensionmark believes advisors who have seen the ups and downs of all market conditions are in a better position to help people. To demonstrate this, Pensionmark did a great job of creating small biographies of each advisor on their website. Each one had a nice picture and a few short paragraphs of copy. We learned where each person went to school. We were informed of any special designation or degree they've earned. And of course, we know exactly how many years they've been in the financial advisory business.

In summary, we got a long list of WHAT these people

have accomplished. What we never saw or felt privy to was what Pensionmark believed.

When my firm was asked to fix Pensionmark's messaging problem, we knew exactly what to do. We created a story they could easily—even gleefully—tell to prospects that started with WHY, not WHAT.

Remember, this is the financial advisory space! Think mahogany desks and brown leather chairs. Stuffy, starched shirts and guys in ties. Not exactly a hotbed of creative thought.

We proposed to Pensionmark a story: a fictional narrative to share a belief. A belief that proves a point—and not just *a* point, but rather *the* point. It went like this:

Imagine you're sitting in an airplane watching a movie on your phone. Suddenly the PA crackles to life. It's the pilot. He says, "Ladies and gentlemen, good afternoon. This is your captain speaking. You'll notice that the flight attendants are coming through to clean the cabin a bit earlier than usual. I just spoke with the control tower and they confirmed what we see here on the radar: There is a big hulk of a storm brewing up ahead.

"The seatbelt sign is on, put your tray table up as soon as possible, because this one is a doozy. I mean, it's probably 200 miles across and growing. Here's the good news: This is a strong aircraft, tough as nails, made of metal by America's finest craftsmen. You should feel comfortable and secure that the plane will be just fine.

"But there is one other thing I want you to know. This is my first commercial flight. I've logged a bunch of hours in the simulator, but this is my first time flying an actual plane. So as you restore your tray tables to an upright position, please say a little prayer on my behalf. A shoutout. You know, a little something-something from the big guy upstairs. I could use some positive juju up here."

You can imagine how terrified you'd be sitting on that plane.

Of course, the Pensionmark advisors had "flown" for decades. They'd seen it all—the turbulence of bear markets, the beautiful horizons of bull markets, and everything in between. We even created animated visuals of a Pensionmark plane flying through the cloudy skies. It was awesome, and we were sure this was a home run.

we *believe*
good pilots
EMBRACE
TURBULENCE

But they didn't want to use the material.

What gives? I'll admit, I'm jealous of the kind of company Pensionmark's founders and leaders have built, and the amazing work they do. We're talking a firm with 20-plus offices across the country and billions in assets under management. Yes, billions.

But no matter how much we pushed the agenda, we couldn't force them to adopt change.

In their minds, it was a confluence of a few different factors. One, they felt it was too hard to fully integrate the new ideas, images, words, and approaches across the various offices.

Two, the narrative was too far outside the scope of everyone else in the industry. People would ridicule them—after all, we're talking about money here. This is serious business. (Remember, people and organizations love to run in herds.)

Three, the effort required outside help in the form of my company. The leaders didn't want to admit they needed help.

Four, we didn't do our job well enough, so they got confused and frustrated.

Regardless of why exactly they didn't adopt our efforts, it was ultimately a wasted effort and a missed opportunity.

You have to break from the herd. I say this with love: fuck the herd. There's safety in thinking like everyone else, but in the safety of the herd, you wind up with no idea where or why you're walking forward. You just follow the safety. Until you run over the cliff.

When you follow the herd, you don't stand for *anything*.

Early in my career, I had a boss who was very influential. You can call him Ron, but I usually just call him Dad. More than anything else, my dad is an artist. For a brief stint, before I was alive, he was a high-school art teacher. Eventually, he moved into the world of advertising and corporate communications. But as a true artisan, he always brought a deep level of emotional awareness and intelligence to every project he touched.

I remember a piece we did for ACNielsen, the ratings company. It was *very* well received, and quickly it seemed like all of our hard work and effort was being scooped up by others. Everyone wanted to claim this "win" as theirs.

My dad said, "Success has many fathers, failure has few." I'll never forget that line.

And you know something? He's right.

When it comes to the deep, foundational, DNA-level stuff like core beliefs, you can't half-ass it. You have to be all the way in. I genuinely believe that you want to maximize profits, make sales, and make your employees happy and successful. You might even be willing to *listen* to outside ideas that actually propel all of that.

But when it comes to implementing those ideas, most people don't do it.

In that case, you're little more than a missed opportunity. And that's what gets under my skin. Because you're better than that. It's painful, and it will take time to fully adopt a core belief—but once you do, it will exponentially improve your company. There's no doubt about it.

You can write the check, listen, and put the phrases on a wall. But until you get behind the wheel and fly the plane, you're just talking.

I want you to fly.

BEAM SUNTORY: THE BEST TRAINWRECK I'VE EVER SEEN

Full warning: I'm about to take my gloves off. Watch out.

A couple years ago, we did an important project with Jim Beam's now-former President of the Americas. The liquor company with a massive global reach, seemingly unlimited resources, and a truckload of cool factor? Yes, *that* Jim Beam.

The president—his name is Tim—had to give a critically important presentation at their annual distributor conference at the Wynn Hotel in Las Vegas along with several VPs and a whole lineup of brand managers. This event was a huge deal. It's the one time each year all their clients (the distributors) are in one room.

Just to give you an idea of the scope: Curtis "50 Cent" Jackson, Mila Kunis, and Justin Timberlake were part of this private, two-and-a-half-day event intended to boost sales of the entire fleet of Jim Beam products. Big bucks, big pressure. That's high stakes if you ask me.

My firm was tasked with making the various keynote presentations nothing less than amazing. I sat down across from Tim, who was still relatively new to the job. It was the first time we'd ever met.

"All right, Tim. You're a year into this thing, and you obviously care. You're the president of one of the most widely recognized brands in the world. Even people who don't drink alcohol know Jim Beam. That's a cool position to be in, actually! Now tell me a little bit about what your firm stands for...what do you guys believe?"

Like most people, C-suite executive or otherwise, he couldn't come close to giving me an answer that made any sense. He talked about what they do and how they do it, but he didn't have a clue why. Of course, this is typical and I had just met the man, so I gave him a free pass.

"What do you think the audience needs to hear from you?" I asked.

"We need more grit. I'm calling it Grit 2.0," he said.

Grit? That wasn't hitting the mark for me, but again, I

gave him a pass. He came from Campbell's Soup, which has a very different sales and distribution model. He was still getting his sea legs in the spirits industry. Surely he'd let me coach him; it's what I do, and it's what they hired us for.

We remained committed. One way or another, we were going to help Tim and his team. But the more we got involved in the project, the more Tim and I started falling apart. We couldn't find much to agree on.

He started saying things like, "You don't understand the audience, Brian." He meant my ideas were too sophomoric for these people. His audience was going to be full of smart, powerful people. People who only need data—otherwise known as bullet-point lists of WHAT.

Quickly, it became clear that Tim just wanted us to be quiet and "clean up his slides."

Yep, right here is when I started to unlace the gloves. Tim was going to get a fight from me. Not because I was that invested in him—remember, I hardly knew him—rather, for the *audience*. They deserved the very best, and that's why my firm was brought in.

He was the president, he was smart, and he was capable— all of that was true. But he didn't have the courage to *not* lean into the default. He didn't understand that his job as president and leader, first and foremost, was to set a strategy and course based on the beliefs of Jim Beam as a company.

He wanted to focus on numbers. For example, they had this green apple whiskey that he wanted to showcase and talk about. The way he talked about it focused on Jim Beam instead of his audience. He told them about an algorithm they used to determine a flavor profile for today's millennial consumer. He told them how amazing the label was. How great the price was. And how successful it was in freakin' Portland. Who cares about Portland?

"People want to know what you stand for. You could even say, 'We believe in the cutting edge. At Jim Beam, we understand that today's consumer is looking to be on the frontlines of trends. People want to be cool, to be first, to be 'in the know.' They use Pinterest and Instagram, where they see new things and satiate their curiosity. They're worldly. They love the old stalwarts, but they also love the adventure in trying new products. Because of that, we've put a team in place to come up with amazing new products that we've tested in places like Portland: introducing, green apple whiskey.'"

It would have been the same message—just different,

and more focused on why. Of course, he refused—flat out *refused* my advice.

Eventually, we found ourselves a week away from the big meeting in Las Vegas. In advance, we were doing a full-blown rehearsal in a supremely adequate hotel ballroom, just north of Chicago. Jim Beam had rented a stage, a teleprompter operator, show director, graphics operators, and a bunch of other brand people were there—maybe 20 people total in the room. Tim and I had (mostly) pleasantly gone toe to toe for weeks up to this point, and I had told him many times that his presentation was missing the core ingredients for success. I predicted it would not maximize the opportunity, and he'd soon regret the structure he created. But he refused to listen. He was the big boss, with full veto power, so the choice was his.

All afternoon, the rehearsals went swimmingly. One by one, individual brand managers were killing it. Using the words, ideas, and structure we created, brands like Knob Creek, Makers Mark, and EFFEN Vodka came alive! We knew what these spirits stood for and how they fit within the Beam family. Everyone in the room knew that as well as these presentations were going, there was really only one that truly mattered...

Tim's.

The audio engineer put a microphone on him. The graphics operator handed him a clicker. The clock, which counts down to zero, was set to 45 minutes, and the director said, "The stage is yours, Tim."

He came to the conclusion of his rehearsal speech and you could hear a pin drop—in a bad way. Even the lighting designer, who had no dog in this fight, looked at me and said, "What the hell was that?"

Nobody said a word to Tim.

All day my job had been to break the silence and give kudos, feedback, additional ideas, and encouragement.

This time, everyone looked at me with anticipation. They all knew how much it missed the mark, but nobody ever wants to deliver that news.

It takes more guts than you can believe, but I remembered the stack of custom T-shirts we had back at the office. A year earlier, I had them printed with this on the front: "Can you handle the ugly truth?"

My job was to help, and my core belief is to make waves. Sometimes, when those two things come together, I have no choice but to offer the ugly truth.

He looked at me, and I didn't mince words: "Well, that was terrible."

He was taken aback.

"Tim, I think we've got some work to do."

"That's just how these presentations go. You don't know this audience." He stormed off the stage and it was clear to everyone, including me, that simply saying, "It was great, Tim" would have been a lot easier. Clearly, I was going to get yelled at first, and fired second.

Sadly, that didn't happen.

Once we got to Vegas, I provided 50 Cent some counsel on his presentation. He's more than a spokesperson for Beam-owned EFFEN Vodka—he's a savvy businessman. 50 knew how to turn on the charm, work the room, and tell people what they wanted to hear. This fact wasn't lost on me when he said, "Dude, who are you? My presentation is so much better now. You the man!"

He took my advice, did a great job on his presentation, and now we're releasing a collaboration album together. (I wish!)

A week later at the Wynn, Tim was getting onstage, about to give a message that was, in theory, worth flying across the country for. After all, that's what these business owners did.

I knew how this was going to unfold, so I didn't watch the stage—I watched the audience. I had the timer on my iPhone ready, and as soon as the voiceover said his name and title—the signal for Tim to hit the stage—I started the clock.

Twenty-seven seconds. That's all it took.

In less than half a minute of the first presentation of the day, made by the senior leader we were supposed to listen to the most, you could see the glow of cellphones illuminating the faces of audience members.

The presentation was selfish, one-sided, and boring. It lacked any meaningful connection to the audience; nothing about it felt up to the magnitude of the event. By four minutes in, I looked at SquarePlanet's chief of design and said, "There's still 41 minutes left."

Luckily for everyone, he burned through his 45 minutes in just a bit more than half an hour.

By the end, people didn't even feign interest, they were openly engaging in their own side conversations. It was a disaster.

Mind you, nobody threw tomatoes at Tim or booed him offstage. They did something much worse: They turned against him and tuned him out. And when you're in a place like Vegas—with every distraction known to man—it's tough enough. But to engage an audience with a deck full of numbers anywhere other than a card table? Good luck.

The point is simple: Get your core belief right at the top because if you don't, the domino effect will keep you from getting it right at the bottom.

We are all prone to errors. We are human beings first, and business leaders second (or maybe even third or fourth). But if you can get a few things right early, it will make a big difference in your company. Sometimes that means you'll have to let go of the old way and try something new. That can be painful—even emotional—and it will challenge who you are and how you perceive yourself, like it did for Tim.

So be more like my good buddy Curtis—you can call him 50 Cent—and take the advice.

It's miserable to die a slow death where your core beliefs don't align with your actions. In that case, you're just another buffalo in the herd and you'll be miserable no matter what.

To me, this is a very big deal. You have to create congruence. Otherwise, you'll be one of those "unlucky" people who had every opportunity in their life to get it right, but just didn't take it.

As my wife likes to say, life is too *long* to get this wrong.

How do you take control of your destiny instead? By implementing your core beliefs, of course. And that's exactly what we'll cover in Part III.

PART III

IMPLEMENTING CORE BELIEFS

CHAPTER 7

CONGRUENCE AND THE CORE BELIEF FILTER

"Defining, embedding, and living core beliefs set the stage for executives and employees to connect. Through actions that consistently convey who we are and how we act, executives can inspire employees to believe in the organization's values and buy in to its brand."

—PUNIT RENJEN

This will sound terrible. It's not, I promise. It's actually a relief:

Your core belief doesn't have to be great—you just have to start with something.

The number of companies that have *anything* is incredibly low, so if you have something that's true to you, that's a great start. But you must implement it.

It can be incredibly simple, like "Think Different." That phrase occupies so many spaces for Apple—everything from music players, to the way they design and build computers, to their conception of the phone. They look at everything through the lens of thinking differently.

Your core belief may not be that simple and straightforward—and it may not be that good at first—but you have to stand for something.

With the goal of trying to find these oftentimes all-too-elusive core beliefs, we've cobbled together a number of mechanisms that lead us to the answer. One simple approach? Ask yourself three questions internally:

What business are we in?

What business are we *really* in?

What business should we be in?

I love this exercise. It forces you to think about your business in a deeper, more purposeful way.

Of course, it's also a classic example of one of those "sounds simple, but is far-from-easy" tasks; I mean, best of luck answering these questions!

At SquarePlanet, we answer the second question by saying we are in the *relationship* business. I deeply, authentically believe in the power of relationships. We want our actions to be personal, purposeful, and impactful. As such, one of our core beliefs is to "make people feel special."

So if we want to act with congruence toward that belief, we have to take some actions. In our case, we created a program and associated processes that we call "PPI." It stands for "personal, purposeful, and impactful."

The PPI program starts with a simple goal: Ideally five times a quarter, we have our antennas up for an important event or milestone in the lives of our clients, partners, and associates. For example, one of our vendor partners—a guy by the name of Scott "Fish" Roberts—told us he and his wife were expecting their first child. We immediately thought, "Here's a chance for a PPI gift," and we put it on the list.

We don't leave any relationship to chance.

Our goal is simple: We want to love on those people closest to us and cement our connection with them. Our relationships are so important to us that we actually budget for PPI gifts! We set aside money for salaries, health insurance, coffee, rent, and a million other things—and yes, 20 PPI gifts per year go into our annual budget projections.

When our vendor, Scott, and his wife, Stephanie, have their baby, we'll send them something. Remember, we make waves, so it won't be a simple onesie from Amazon. It will be something customized with the baby's name on it or a logo with Scott's favorite sports team (in Scott's case, the Miami Dolphins, thus the nickname "Fish")— something truly purposeful and meaningful to them. One thing's for sure: The gift will also include a handwritten note on custom SquarePlanet stationery. We'll wait a while after the child's birth to send it, too.

Why?

Think about the flipside of a birth: when someone dies. There's always a flood of people bringing over food, cards, and flowers to the family. Instead, I think you should wait a few months for all the attention and spotlight to come to a grinding halt. Then, out of nowhere, send a gift: "I brought you a pan of lasagna, because I've been thinking about you and hoping you're OK." That's a gesture with real impact.

The point is, we are mindful about having a process to track and follow up on our clients' important life events, which is a direct extension of our core beliefs. Seriously, it's a process. We have a file structure set up that lists what was sent to whom, and when. We have nice gift boxes, ribbons, tissue paper, and stationery on a shelf of our storeroom so there's no scrambling for the necessary accouterment to execute on a PPI.

Make no mistake, we're not trying to buy our way to a solid relationship. That's just stupid and won't work in the long run. No, what we're doing is authentically acting on a core belief. And those on the receiving end love it! They remember how we made them feel, and because we come from a place of honest commitment to our relationships, they know what we did wasn't cursory. In fact, it's exactly the opposite. Why? Because the gesture we decide on is *personal, purposeful, and impactful*.

The point is, all of your actions must be run through the filter of your core belief. If you don't, you risk incongruence in your company, which can tear you down over time.

A BAD WAITRESS AT THE FOUR SEASONS

Imagine you're staying at the Four Seasons. You walk in and the first thing you notice is how beautiful the air smells (they pump in a signature scent through the ventilation system, you know). Then the employees go out of their way to grab your bag and lighten your load. Luxury and beauty permeate everything.

Then you sit down to lunch at the hotel restaurant.

You ask for a sweet tea.

The waitress says, "We have regular iced tea, but I can bring you sugar."

You say, "Actually, I want a premade sweet tea. It's different."

And the waitress says, "Well that's not how we do it," and gives you a dismissive attitude.

All she'd have to do is go back to the bar, ask the bartender for a bit of simple syrup, and make the sweet tea. Doing that would be totally congruent with the rest of your experience, since it aligns with the core belief of "exceptional service" that Four Seasons is known for. Instead, you're left wondering why this person works here in the first place.

Sure, she's probably a capable server. But her beliefs don't match the Four Seasons. She might be better off at one of those *Dick's Last Resort* restaurants where they are purposefully caustic, make rude jokes at your expense, and put silly paper hats on your head. I love those places!

But the Four Seasons isn't Dick's Last Resort.

Rooted in their core belief, the Four Seasons aims to

pamper their guests. They want to lighten your burden at every turn. But in this case, I guess that doesn't include sweet tea.

And that's what incongruence looks like—it looks and feels like mixed messages. In an isolated incident, it just feels annoying. On an organizational, long-term level, it looks like the complete breakdown of your organization's key message (McDonald's, anyone?).

> It's like asking two people for directions and both of them tell you to go the opposite way—if you're in a new town, which one do you believe?

Typically there's nothing malicious about incongruence. You might not be intentionally acting without congruence—but the effect of this is just the same. You *confuse* your customers.

WHEN IT'S TIME TO GO

Without fail, after every speech or presentation I give, there is a line of people who want to speak with me. I love this part. Oh sure, it's great for my ego—but more importantly, I can't wait to hear what they have to say. I always get a great new nugget of information or a deeper insight I can use for other projects. The collective wisdom of the audience is very real.

Invariably, however, somewhere toward the back of the line, there's one person who asks the same question as many other back-of-the-liners before them. And I always see it coming, perhaps it's the tears in their eyes. Every time it's the same, they say:

"What if my personal beliefs are different than my company's core beliefs? What do I do?"

"I can see the emotion written all over your face. You already know what you need to do. You need to find a place that believes what you believe."

It's hard for people. What they realize is that, as human beings, they are entitled to their own set of individual beliefs, and that's a great thing. But companies are entitled to that, too. So if your beliefs don't line up, it's time for one of you to decide to move on. Otherwise, you risk damaging everything by creating incongruence.

MONEY OVER RELATIONSHIPS
AT TRANSAMERICA

Transamerica created a retirement division that was built by a lot of people who were incredibly focused on the humanity of what they were doing, both internally and externally. They helped people get ready for retirement, and that was meaningful work for these people.

The organization was built by leaders who wanted to inspire and motivate. They did so with a warm embrace, a pat on the back, and a can-do attitude that could get you through dark times.

Then, their leadership changed. All of a sudden, it became more about the bottom line and hitting more aggressive quarterly goals, than creating human relationships. If you were a hardworking person and had a bad year? Whoo, buddy, you were still in trouble.

For many people who had built legacies at Transamerica, they felt betrayed. This had been a place that shared their values, beliefs, and mission to help people with their financial future. The place became corporate and incredibly data-driven. It lost its humanity, and that incongruence meant there were people questioning if they should work there.

In fact, many people simply left. They understood that it's a business and it has to be profitable, but it was a much less human-centered approach. So they hit the road, Jack.

Without congruence, your best people leave.

That's why about 70 percent of the workforce sucks.

According to a decades-long survey by Gallup, about 50

percent of employees are either neutral or numb to the company's expressed purpose and goals; about 20 percent actively work *against* it; and 30 percent are actively and positively engaged. This final group is key, as they make the company go.

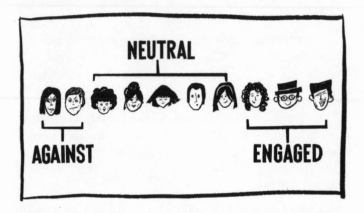

Those 30 percent have congruence with what the company stands for. The other 70 percent are just there for a paycheck.

Yes, I'm painting with a broad brush here and I joke about all of those people sucking, but it is at least *somewhat* true. And frankly, it's possible the 70 percent just don't know the organization's core beliefs. It's hard to act in accordance with something you don't know.

Imagine if you could get your organization's core beliefs in order? Imagine if your website, marketing presentations, mission statement, and the spoken words of everyone from senior leaders down to the most junior-level hourly employee were completely congruent?

> Granted, you will never get all 70 percent of the disengaged to come to your side. And once you more effectively communicate your core beliefs, you will face backlash from that 70 percent. The pain will be real, disruptive, and scary. But if you can move even a small percentage (say, 10 percent of that 70 percent) to congruence, you will see massive effects to your bottom line. In other words, it's now 40 percent of your staff making the organization go. That's a lot more horsepower! And if you drive some of them away, so be it. The goal is to work with people who believe what you believe.

Imagine Apple has a bunch of people who say, "You know what? Screw thinking different. The phone is exactly what it's always been: It has a dial, and you have a cord at the end of it. We're not going to think different."

That kind of thinking could crush the entire operation. Everything would become combative. It would become a fight to change anything.

You could have the most benign belief in the world, but if you scream it loudly enough, someone will fight against it. Welcome the fight. It means you're on to something.

HOW DO YOU ENSURE CONGRUENCE WITH A CORE BELIEF?

You bake it into everything your organization does. And I do mean *everything*.

Become a fanatic. Everything you do must be through the lens of your beliefs—that's first and foremost.

You can't just shout your beliefs to your clients, then do something else internally. No. You have to create processes that implement actions that are congruent with core beliefs.

For example, at SquarePlanet, we have those PPIs I mentioned earlier. Likewise, for onboarding, every new employee sits with me and I walk them through our full history. Then they have a variety of meetings with people in the organization, including other people who teach them what they need to start their job. It's all built in for every new person, and we take it very seriously.

Shift7 does the same thing. They put together a process for engineered delight, for associates, current customers, and potential customers alike. They don't leave anything to chance, so they built out a process.

On their intake form, they ask questions about your birthday and other events, so they can capitalize and send you personalized gifts on important days. They even do little things. For example, if they have a new business pitch with a potential client at 4 p.m., they ask for access to the room at 3 p.m. In that hour, they transform the space with Shift7 signage in order to transport their audience to a different place spatially. And it's not just one rep who decides to do this stuff every once in a while. Every team member does it every time. That transformation is baked into their *actions* because it's baked into their beliefs.

Ritz-Carlton, for example, has such a simple and brilliant process to delight customers. If you roll up to a Ritz hotel, the doorman will say, "Good afternoon, sir. May I ask the party's name?"

"Burkhart, party of two."

Then they immediately get on their little secret-service radio-com system and say to the front desk, "The Burkharts are coming to the front desk. He's wearing a blue blazer and she's got on a yellow sweater."

Then, as you walk up to the front desk agent, they magically say, "Mr. Burkhart, welcome to the Ritz-Carlton. We're glad you're here."

What the? How the hell did they know my name? DUH! The dude outside asked for it like 20 seconds ago. They have a remarkably simple system built in that ensures congruence around delighting the customer every single time.

The key here is that you can articulate the crystal-clear belief, but if you don't implement processes that derive from that core belief, you run the risk of incongruence in action.

Even though I know (and even expect) the Ritz-Carlton to delight me in this way, I still love it. So will your customers and clients, if you take the time to turn your core beliefs into actions that delight them.

> The process and actions themselves can change and evolve over time as your organization evolves. That's natural. But the core beliefs that drive those processes will remain evergreen.

EMPLOYEE EDUCATION

What is nurtured, grows.

Sorry, I hate to tell you this, but core beliefs are not "set-it-and-forget-it" kind of work. As you add people, you can't assume that because you created a core belief two years ago, people will magically learn it. You have to continually educate people on how to act on these beliefs within your organization.

The best organizations get together and talk about this stuff on a regular basis. At SquarePlanet, we do what we call "Highs and Lows." We have a little red Moroccan fez hat with the tassel on the end, and in that hat, we have pieces of paper with everyone's names. We all sit around the conference table and pull a name out of the hat. If your name gets pulled, you have to tell the group a high and a low since the last time we had one of these meetings. It can be a combination of personal and professional highs and lows, too—it's a safe place to come clean about things that have been on your chest in a negative way, and a good way to give praise to people and talk about things you're proud of.

The only rule is that it always has to come back to one of our core beliefs. So when someone does something that they're proud of, I always connect it to our core beliefs in action.

It's small stuff—and it's seemingly inconsequential—but those little processes, those little meetings, and those little training materials will all add up to a greater level of congruence.

And I know what you're thinking...this is a great idea for a small team, but what about a BIG team? Well, the truth is, group size doesn't matter. Consider the "Highs and Lows" idea on a grand scale. It's absolutely possible.

Imagine a large group where each team member sends a text message to a single number. The message is that person's high or low and the leader goes through the list, randomly picking out messages to discuss.

It may not be intimate or deeply personal, but the idea would help generate the congruence around beliefs you may be looking for.

ASCENSUS: SEMIANNUAL TUNE-UPS

Jason used to work for Transamerica, but he left during the great exodus and went to a firm called Ascensus. He's a true leader—people often say they would walk through fire for him. Which is great because he leads the national sales team, and he strongly believes that ongoing education is key to building a top-tier sales team. And let me tell you, Jason is as smart as they come. As such, he wants his own team to be razor sharp, so he puts them to the test using twice-yearly "tune-ups."

The tune-ups go like this: At their national meeting, individual sales reps get onstage and for ten minutes, they educate the audience about a prepared topic. There is a clock visible to both the presenter and the audience, counting down from ten minutes to zero with a hard-stop buzzer at the end. All your colleagues are watching, so is senior leadership, and the topics aren't easy. This is high-pressure stuff.

It serves two purposes. First, it's an opportunity for individual sales reps to offer their best practices on a topic and educate each other. Second, it gives Jason a chance to see who's really got their shit figured out—to see who's going rogue and who's sticking to the core beliefs of the firm. In short, in a limited amount of time, this exercise sharpens everyone's skills and informs Jason about the skillset of his team.

It all goes back to Jason's core belief that the best sales teams are continuously educated. He didn't choose to get onstage and yammer away for eight hours straight (which he's highly capable of doing). Instead, he decided to construct quick, 10-minute sessions, presented by a large portion of the total sales team to challenge and teach each other.

Moreover, he doesn't go to the best cold-caller and tell them to give a presentation on cold calling. He'll stick the cold-calling expert on another topic, forcing them to dive deep and learn something new.

Keep in mind: none of this is an easy choice. It would be easy for Jason to say, "Let's only get a handful of the top performers onstage." It's more work for Jason to include and direct a larger sample set of sales reps. It's a hard choice, but ultimately, it's the choice most tied to his and his firm's core beliefs.

Maybe you don't set up semiannual tune-ups like Jason. Maybe you believe your team should be rewarded and have fun. It might be as simple as scheduling a few bowling nights or baseball games to act in congruence with your core beliefs. Whatever it is, just remember to actually do it!

TIESTA TEA: LIVING LOOSE

Tiesta Tea, which I mentioned in Chapter 1, is all about living loose, which they do by selling loose leaf tea. They believe in enjoying life and making it full of rituals.

Fueled by the growth of the business, Dan, Pat, and their team have enjoyed more opportunities—like creating a ready-to-drink, pre-bottled tea for Target. With those opportunities, they have to ask themselves: Is a pre-bottled product *incongruent* with our core belief based around loose? And what about the larger question of how to embrace change and new opportunities, and yet still be congruent with your core beliefs?

In their case, they brewed and bottled the drink in a facility using only loose leaf tea, and they communicated that on their packaging.

They could have stayed locked into their processes and actions over time, and stubbornly clung to the idea that pre-bottled tea went against their beliefs—even if it really didn't. They had the courage to break free of their processes, and allowed the *manifestation* of that core belief to change, but the belief itself never did.

DRIVING ON AUTOPILOT

When you first started driving as a teenager, you had to think about it. You actively thought about how to position your seat; securing your seatbelt with a robust click; where your hands would go; using your mirrors; and maybe even setting the perfect temperature. It was all a conscious thought process.

After you've been driving long enough, you've undoubtedly become more comfortable. In fact, I bet at some point you've driven from Point A to Point B—probably from work to your house—and suddenly found yourself walking through your front door wondering, "Whoa. How did I get home? I don't remember the drive at all."

And yet, somehow, you safely navigated a fast-moving, 3,000-pound vehicle to your driveway. It just *happened*.

Living authentically through your core beliefs is a lot like that. At first, it will be a conscious process you have to force yourself to stick with. It's going to feel awkward and yucky. But over time, you won't even think about it. You'll just make waves, or build relationships, or think different, or build from the backseat forward, or make soap without chemicals, or make tasty cheeseburgers and not carrot muffins.

I promise you, the longer you embrace your core beliefs, the easier it will get.

Everything I've discussed in this chapter is relatively simple and easy to do. The processes necessary to implement your core beliefs and create congruence can be incredibly simple, as long as they're thought out and intentional. In fact, in many ways, the most successful congruence processes *are* the simplest.

If you're consistent with them over time, and intentional, your core beliefs will permeate everything you do. In other words, you will lead with your core beliefs.

CHAPTER 8

HOW TO LEAD WITH BELIEFS

"Good business leaders create a vision, articulate the vision, passionately own the vision, and relentlessly drive it to completion."

—JACK WELCH

It was a typical networking event, nothing particularly unusual or high stakes about it.

So why was I so nervous?

The host simply said, "Let's go around the room. Please introduce yourself, tell us what you do, and just do a quick little intro."

I'm incredibly comfortable presenting onstage in front of thousands of people. Onstage is where I feel strongest. Not acting, mind you—that's never been a thing for me. Rather, presenting my ideas and being the authentic me— that's my happy place. Yet at this dinky little Chamber of Commerce event, I could feel my heart ripping through my chest cavity in anticipation of answering those simple questions in front of 50 people.

One by one, I heard people say their names and what they do.

"Kerri Schneider, and I operate a financial firm."

"Kevin Washington, and I am the VP of sales for an OEM manufacturer."

As my turn approached, I knew I'd have to make a choice. I could follow the herd and say *what* I did, or

I could break from the status quo and stand for something, and say *why*.

I stood up, not knowing if I'd follow through or not.

The adrenaline pumped through my bloodstream, and oh was my heart racing! I could feel butterflies in my belly, something I hadn't felt since my wedding day. SquarePlanet was a new company, and I'd only recently put words to our core beliefs. I didn't have the comfort of an entire process and organization of people around me to say all of this with certainty. This was brand new to me, and my choice here could change how I viewed my company forever.

Mind you, there was a very low possibility that I'd ever work with any of these people; established data around new business development indicates they probably wouldn't become clients. But I was about to define the story I told myself about my organization. Would nerves get the best of me? Would I back down from leading with my beliefs, or would I stand for something and start to create a brand people love?

"Hi, I'm Brian and I believe in making waves—of course, that's not of the aquatic variety. We help our clients elevate their most important messages, so people remember and act on them. My firm is called SquarePlanet and we love the color orange. Thanks!"

I sat down. People turned around and watched me. People who weren't paying attention before gave me this look of interest and intrigue.

I barely noticed as the next half of the room each said their piece. Then, once all 50 people had gone, the host turned to me *first* and said, "Brian, what was it you do?"

"I make waves."

"Tell us more about that. I'm intrigued."

Fifty smart, experienced, capable, hardworking people just described *what* they do, yet I'm the one who captured her interest. I stood out in a room full of people who know business. And it wasn't because I'm handsome like Channing Tatum, or as big as Shaquille O'Neal, or as strong as Dwayne 'The Rock" Johnson. I'm Captain Vanilla, Joe Average, Johnny Normal. So why did she call on me to elaborate on what I do?

Because I told them something different than everyone else: *I told them what I believed.*

If I had compromised in that moment and said, "You know what? I don't want to make a fool of myself. My company's new," it would have been so much easier to compromise in future moments as well. Once you get past those first few initial hurdles, you'll realize that nobody will laugh at you. Nobody will throw tomatoes at you. Nobody.

On the surface, it seems like a piece of cake. But leading with your beliefs is hard...I get it. I've been there.

Here I am, Mr. Put-Me-In-Front-Of-1,000-People-And-I'll-Talk-For-An-Hour-No-Problem, but when someone asked me to say my name and what I do, I was ready to die.

That's how painful this stuff is.

LEAD WITH BELIEFS

Your old brain wants you to stay safe. It wants you to stay in the herd.

But it also wants you to latch onto a why.

There's a reason why people have a hard time articulating why they do things—it's because language is formed in the new brain, and that's separate from the old brain. Simply put, your brain isn't wired to find the words around why, so it's easier to lead with what and disconnect the why. But why has the power to draw consumers in and lead them to your what.

Remember that Subaru commercial from the Introduction? The "Backseat Anthem" with the most valuable real estate on Earth? Their marketing team may not have been thinking about leading with why, or using the old brain first—but that's what they did, and it wasn't an accident. They didn't intrigue you by saying all the features they offer. They connected you to their why first, then got to the how and what.

HOW TO LEAD WITH WHY

First and foremost, you must get the basics right. Odds are, you're trying to make things too complex. Look at your business cards, your website, and even your outgoing phone message and email signature.

Your out-of-office message represents an opportunity here. It's easy to say, "I'll be out of the office from Tuesday until Friday. Please call this number if you have an emergency." It's not wrong—but it could be better.

Compare with this: "I believe in restorative time with the closest and most important people in my world: my family. While I love you too, and you're super important to me, I'm taking five days to ignore you. If there's a real-deal emergency, call my assistant at this number. See you in a week."

Remember, you're speaking to other human beings. People who share the same needs, wants, pains, hopes, dreams, etc. as you. Stop believing this kind of message may make you look unprofessional or weak. Just imagine if you received it, how would you feel about the sender?

It's better and more engaging...because it's human, and humans should lead with beliefs.

I'm willing to guess nearly 99 percent of organizations and people lead with *whats*. Before you can get comfortable leading with why, you need to get comfortable saying it outwardly in those basic, simple ways. So, start there.

What we've found, however, is that people have a hard time standing in front of a group of people and starting with why—whether it's with slides or in a Chamber of Commerce meeting. To combat this, we created something called the sidewinder technique that I think you're really gonna like.

THE SIDEWINDER TECHNIQUE

The idea here is to ultimately take the deeply held beliefs you keep as a company and express them in a story. It's a unique, unexpected, simple way of getting a core message across without the anxiety of being so upfront about it.

This is what we gave Pensionmark with the experienced-pilot metaphor. It's powerful because it's actually fun, illustrative, and keeps the attention of your audience.

We did something similar for Y Media Labs, a Bay Area technology company that faced a common problem: Potential customers often don't understand the complex language of technology.

After spending some time in San Francisco with the people at Y Media, we realized they were a tough group. And by tough, I mean they were grinders. No matter what, the gang at Y Media would never give in, never give up. No deadline too daunting, no technology issue that can't be resolved.

That led my team to craft a remarkable core belief delivered in a single line: *Yield to Nothing.*

It worked so well because the entire focus of the company was to make elegant, engaging solutions. More often than not, that meant apps. At the time, apps were hot—as in "surface-of-the-sun" hot. Every brand (big or small) thought the key to customer retention and increased revenue was building an app.

But these potential customers didn't really speak app. They didn't know what they needed or wanted, had no idea how the technology actually worked, and certainly didn't have a clue how to build any of it. And let's face it, nobody wants to feel stupid. So we figured, "Let's showcase Y Media's core belief while simultaneously meeting the client where they are."

To do so, we came up with a thick notecard. One side of the card had a bunch of technobabble written on it. It was legit information regarding the construction of an app, but it's Greek to 99.8 percent of the public. Then there was another overlay card, which worked like a filtering spy-decoder lens that revealed the message with the core belief of Y Media Labs spelled out.

A MOBILE APP IS COMPUTER PROGRAM DESIGNED TO RUN ON MOBILE DEVICES SUCH AS SMARTPHONES AND TABLETS. SIMPLY PUT, A MOBILE APP IS SOMETHING YOU CAN USE 'ON THE GO'. SOMETIMES MOBILE APPS ARE DEVELOPED FOR PURPOSES OF ENTERTAINMENT. SOMETIMES BUSINESSES CREATE APPS SO THAT THEIR CUSTOMERS CAN PURCHASE AND INTERACT WITH THEIR PRODUCT. SOME APPS ARE AMAZING, THEY BECOME SO ENGRAINED AS A PART OF OUR DAILY LIVES THAT WE BECOME UNSURE HOW WE EVER LIVED WITHOUT IT. WHATEVER THE GOAL OF THE APP, USER FUNCTIONALITY SHOULD ALWAYS BE A PRIORITY DURING THE DEVELOPMENT PROCESS. THERE ARE MANY FACTORS THAT MUST BE TAKEN INTO CONSIDERATION DURING THE DEVELOPMENT OF A MOBILE SOLUTION. THESE FACTORS INCLUDE AMOUNT AND VARYING SIZE OF DISPLAY SCREENS, HARDWARE SPECIFICATIONS AS WELL AS AN ARRAY OF TECHNICAL CONFIGURATIONS. MOBILE DEVELOPMENT TEAMS ARE MADE UP OF SEVERAL DIFFERENT SPECIALIZED TEAM MEMBERS, EACH WITH VARYING BACKGROUNDS AND SKILLSETS. WHEN AN APP IS OPENED, WHAT THE USER IS SEEING IS THE CREATION OF USER INTERFACE AND USER EXPERIENCE DESIGNERS (OFTEN SHORTENED TO UI AND UX). THERE ARE ALSO TYPICALLY SEPARATE TEAMS OF ENGINEERS, WHO HAVE AN AMAZINGLY FOCUSED ABILITY TO BRING THESE DESIGNS TO LIFE. IN TERMS OF COLLABORATION, MOST APPS ENDURE AN EXTENSIVE TESTING PROCESS IN WHICH THINGS MIGHT BE CHANGED AND ALTERED DEPENDING ON THE RESULTS OF THAT TESTING. FOR EXAMPLE, IF AN APP ISN'T SAVING INFORMATION CORRECTLY, QUALITY ASSURANCE REPRESENTATIVES WILL TYPICALLY BRING THE PROBLEM TO THE ATTENTION OF AN ENGINEER TO ADDRESS AND ATTEMPT TO FIX. DATA STORAGE ISSUES ARE USUALLY DUE TO ERRORS IN BACK-END DEVELOPMENT, ALTHOUGH SOMETIMES THEY CAN BE ROOTED IN OTHER PLACES. PROJECT MANAGERS ALSO PLAY A CRITICAL ROLE, AS THEY OVERSEE THE ENTIRETY OF THE PROJECT FROM START TO FINISH. IT'S REALLY QUITE SIMPLE.

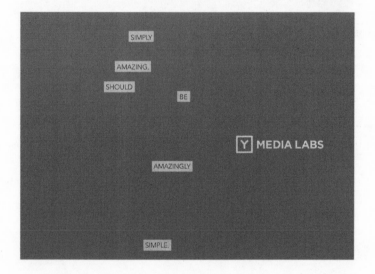

From the outside, you could say these sidewinder techniques—creating materials like the spy decoder, or the stories about flying planes as experienced pilots—are all marketing gimmicks. Even if that were true, or if you believed that, you could still use *real* stories to showcase your beliefs.

You can and should use customer stories in your marketing. They are highly engaging, emotional, and showcase the human connections you make.

WHAT ABOUT BEYOND THE BASICS?

If you are an adult who goes to events like a family Thanksgiving dinner, a cocktail party, or a networking event, eventually you'll be faced with the question, "What do you do for a living?"

You could give the easy answer and say *what* you do. But in that moment, you have an opportunity to take it a cut deeper, by powering through the awkwardness, and lead with your belief.

Sure, it's possible to know your belief on an intellectual level, but when you get face-to-face with someone, it gets real and it gets scary.

How do you answer?

Imagine you work at Nike and someone asks you what you do.

"I work at Nike."

"Oh, that must be cool. Do you get free shoes?"

Now imagine they ask you what you do, and you say, "I honor athletes and athletics."

"I'm sorry, what do you do?"

"I honor athletes and athletics. I do that by helping curate one of the most valuable brands in the world. We work with the latest and greatest technology on feet, apparel, and equipment, to help the best athletes in the world be even better. I work at Nike."

That's a hard conversation because you're worried you'll sound a little crazy. But if you can do it once, and continually over time, you'll build up the strength and conviction you need to shout your belief out loud.

Same thing goes for the interview process. Ask your candidates for examples of times they acted in accordance with your beliefs.

For me, I ask candidates for a time they bucked the trend or did something outside the norm. It could be taking a gap year after college or saying no to a manager's request—show me a time you "made waves."

Great companies that lead with beliefs will use the interviews to get information about the prospect's potential as a culture fit.

This can even seep into your onboarding, policies, and employee handbook. For example, from Day 1, we tell our employees in the handbook that they can get a "bunion bonus." It's ridiculous, but also simple and fun: If they can provide photographic evidence of them rubbing the feet of their significant other's grandparent or parent, I'll give them 50 bucks. It's insane.

It's a policy that tells people how we roll around here. I get to tell them the story of a former employee named Derek, and the origin story around the bunion bonus. It tells the newest team member who we are and what we believe: We are a bit crazy, we are unusual, and we have fun.

If you're not down with that, no problem. Better to know now than later.

YOU SHOULD BE A LITTLE CRAZY

Your commitment to your core beliefs can even inform your office decor. Which Wich has black and yellow colors everywhere in their downtown Dallas office. Once you get off on the 10th floor of their building, you instantly know you've been magically transported to Which Wich Land.

Here's how Jeff, the owner of Which Wich, does it: He has policies in place that ensure the offices are only decorated with black and yellow, Which Wich colors. For example, if you have a picture of your family, your dog, or your favorite beach, you can bring the pic to the coordinator and Jeff, the founder, will personally pay for a uniform black and gold wood frame. It's the exact same frame throughout the office; everyone has it.

He doesn't do this because he's got OCD or because he's a jerk. Quite the opposite. It's because his core belief is that the experience with every restaurant should be the same in look, feel, and sandwich—and that goes as deep as the aesthetic of the corporate office.

And every single employee wears black and yellow every single day—I'm talking shoes, socks, pants, shirts—you name it. If you don't have the money to outfit yourself in those colors, Jeff will give you the clothes off his back. I'm serious. He'll literally outfit you. Jeff believes in the power of a team, and in his mind, teams wear uniforms. It's a seemingly small thing that helps them shout their beliefs and stand for what they believe.

At its deepest level, leading with your core beliefs borders on crazy.

You ever seen those guys shouting Bible verses through a megaphone? Or the person telling you about aliens coming to steal your brain? Yeah, those people have no problem shouting their beliefs, that's for sure. But often, they're a 10 out of 10 on the crazy scale.

I just want you to go to a 9.9.

You will upset some people. I've received plenty of emails from people after they've read one of our job posts saying, "Who do you think you are? I'd NEVER work there." Perfect! Exactly what I was looking to accomplish.

Conversely, you'll draw another group of people toward you: "This is the job of my dreams, you MUST hire me."

Remember, you're trying to create separation on purpose. You only want to work with those who share your beliefs!

> ## DON'T AGITATE FOR THE SAKE OF IT
>
> Of course, you don't want to seek out agitation explicitly, you should just be willing to accept the side effects of shouting your core beliefs. Be true to who you are. If some people agree, awesome. If some people don't, that's awesome, too—that means you're doing it right.

IMAGINE AND BELIEVE

In any language, the two most powerful words are imagine and believe—they are a one-two punch. Use them freely when you communicate your core beliefs.

Whether you're creating videos or blog posts, brochure copy or slide decks, using those words as tools will make for a successful communication strategy.

IMAGINE

Here's how I explain this:

Think back to a time when you read a book, then later it became a movie. Which one did you like better?

Almost invariably, the answer is the book. The reason is

that when you read the book, you were completely in control of imagining what it looked like, sounded like, and felt like. You built a world in your head based on the words. But when you go to the movie, you see someone else's imagination at work, and it almost always fails in comparison.

That's the power of your own imagination—it's more powerful to you than even the best cinematic interpretation of your favorite book.

BELIEVE

Using the word believe is so defining because once you know what your core belief is, you can authentically say, "We / I believe ___."

It's powerful because the notion that we believe anything at all *defines who we are as humans*. That's big. As in *life-altering* big.

We define ourselves in a wide variety of ways. From the way we look, to the status we crave, and the things we do... and what we believe.

Personally, I believe in making waves, accepting blame, delivering the truth, we only get one planet so be nice to it, women can do anything, love is love, and there is no place for hate in any form.

Imagine your own future, one in which you know exactly what you believe, and you have the courage to stand up for it and shout it to the world. How would you feel? What would that life feel like?

One of the financial firms I work with sells 401(k)s to small business owners. These business owners take a tremendous amount of pride in both their business and the employees they employ. Those owners listen when the financial firm says things like, "Imagine a workforce of people who are financially educated and stable, able to take care of themselves over the long haul, and believe in making their own nests, feathered by their own efforts. We believe you, as the business owner, have that unique power. We're here to help you."

They've used language that defines their business by using believe and imagine in both tactful and powerful ways.

Once again, the key to success here is that this can't be bullshit. It can be aspirational, yes, but obvious untruths will do you in. For example, you shouldn't say, "Imagine being 100 pounds thinner. Well, we believe that sucking on grapefruit skin alone will help you lose weight." It has to pass the sniff test. That means it must be real, and it should be emotionally driven.

STRYKER IMPLANTS: MORE THAN DATA FOR THE DOCTORS

Stryker is the largest manufacturer of titanium parts for hip and knee replacements in the world. One of their head honchos is a man named Dr. Richard Conn, and he's spectacular at his job. In short, he gives presentations to groups of doctors and softly sells them on Stryker's products.

Dr. Conn is an accomplished orthopedic surgeon himself. He's a teddy bear of a guy; the doc oozes charm, especially when he fires up his signature Southern drawl. All of this makes him easy to underestimate, but Dr. Conn is sly like a fox. Spend even a few minutes with him and very quickly, you'll realize he's the real deal.

The manner in which he presented to other surgeons, however, remained unchanged for some time—until of course the *make waves* guy came onto the scene. Traditionally, Dr. Conn filled his slides with charts and graphs—and if he wanted to spice things up, pictures of medical procedures. This is known as a data dump. He focused on the *what*: the efficacy of their products, what the specific malady was, how many of their patients they improved, and how quickly they healed. Doctors are scientists, yes, so they are fans of data—data helps tell a story and prove a point.

And these are not dumb people by any stretch—they're surgeons who chop out your bones and replace them with titanium parts—but they're humans, too. Just like anyone else, they get bored with a bunch of data points that defy a well-coalesced narrative.

Unlike Dr. Conn, his presentations had no personality, no connection, and no storyline to draw them in.

There was no *why*.

It was actually quite simple for Dr. Conn to fix his presentations. He started telling stories and using parallels that were unexpected and showed why these procedures mattered so much: "Here's Joe. He was on the fast track to the Olympic team for downhill skiing when he shattered most of his left leg. I promised him we'd get him walking without a limp."

I mean, we even worked in custom motion graphics for allusions like "Whack-A-Mole" to describe problems that kept popping up. This stuff was a far cry from his bullet points and data dumps of old.

But really, none of the above is actually the point. See, here's the thing: Dr. Conn is no spring chicken. He's one of the pioneers of CJR (complete joint replacement) orthopedic surgery. In fact, it's rumored he has been an orthopedic surgeon for so long that he did a hip replacement on a T-Rex.

Imagine what it must have been like for him when I showed up on the scene. Suddenly, this loud-mouthed Yankee who's got zero medical background is telling him there's a better way of doing it.

Let's face it: you'd be skeptical, too.

He may have thought my approach was as likely to float worse than a rock in water, but he also had a hunch that this might make sense. That changing his presentation and taking a risk might work out for him. That there was value in taking a more *human* approach to his work.

Together, we got the message right—but as much as anything, it was Dr. Conn's commitment and willingness to try something new, and to stick with it. The point is, he knew full well that he was going to be in front of his peers, doing something totally foreign, yet he fought through. He stuck it out. He actually did it.

This stuff takes a degree of brass of the highest order. It might make all the logical sense in the world, but once you stand in front of a room full of people staring back at you, you have to be able to handle the heat.

Dr. Conn enthusiastically jumped into the fire, and he absolutely crushed it.

Truthfully, it's hard to tell if his efforts resulted in huge profit gains for Stryker, but the anecdotal evidence is overwhelming. Dr. Conn reported greater audience engagement, more audience participation, and more questions after every presentation. Plus, he felt great. He enjoyed the role and responsibility in a much bigger way.

The lesson is simple: be bold! Take risks. You may think you have to embody a certain detached style, specifically in the business world. Wrong. We've been socialized to play it safe, right down the middle, following the herd, and leading with WHAT and HOW.

I'm telling you to do the opposite. You have to have courage to stand in front of a room like a group of scientists and doctors who demand data points and connect with them emotionally. Trust me: It's worth it.

> In the absence of direction, people will absolutely automatically focus on what and how. That's corporate America today. Just listen to people the next time they have to introduce themselves at work. That's the herd mentality. You want your team to hide in the herd? Be my guest.
>
> You want something more? Stand for something.

INDEPENDENCE REQUIRES RISK

Seriously, you might be in for some deep, emotional work.

Consider the long line of people throughout history who stood up for what they believed: Muhammad Ali, Ruth Bader Ginsburg, Lenny Bruce, Joan of Arc, the Dalai Lama, Colin Kaepernick, Elon Musk, Pablo Picasso, Jane Goodall, Steve Jobs, Jackie Robinson.

For me, there are two others that always come to mind. The first is the unknown man who, in 1989, stood toe to toe with a column of tanks in China's Tiananmen Square. The other is Mahatma Gandhi. This slightly built man stood up to the largest military force in the world at the time, the British Empire. He risked his life to tell the world what he stood for: The Indian subcontinent should be independent of British imperialism.

He started a revolution. And he did it at great risk, as did the unknown man in China.

There is no way around this: You're going to have to stand up and take a risk. And you might think I'm overselling it by comparing your quest with Gandhi's, but I don't think so. It may not be for the independence of your country, but you absolutely have the power to change lives. Including (and especially) your own in a really honest, meaningful way.

If you stand up, then stand out, and tell people what you're all about, there's a pretty good chance it will have both negative and positive impacts. You will drive people away and pull others in closer.

The people who make a dent in the universe will inevitably alienate people. That's just how it goes.

So do you wanna make some waves with me? Remember, fortune favors the bold!

CHAPTER 9

WORK WITH THOSE WHO BELIEVE WHAT YOU BELIEVE

"The goal is not to do business with everybody who needs what you have. The goal is to do business with people who believe what you believe."

—SIMON SINEK

Let me paint a picture for you. The interior of an REI store is a sight to behold. You walk into a large big-box retail store that looks and feels like a campground. It's incredible. They have canoes, racks of mountain bikes, CamelBaks, tents, sleeping bags, fishing poles, hiking boots, and everything else you could possibly need to enjoy the outdoors.

My wife and I live in Phoenix, Arizona, where on average—107 days of the year—the temperature exceeds

100 degrees Fahrenheit. It's widely known for dry, arid conditions. When enjoying outdoor activities like hiking or bike riding, hydration is key. Actually, it's life or death.

No surprise, the CamelBak is a big seller in these parts. Essentially, it's a highly engineered, perfectly balanced backpack with a water bladder built inside. During the summer months, you wouldn't consider hiking without one. And we're talking three liters of water here—that's a lot of liquid in one space! All comfortably and conveniently built into a CamelBak backpack.

There are a few knockoff versions of the CamelBak, but none as good as the original created by parent company Vista Brands.

A publicly traded company, Vista Brands—like most businesses—is focused on profits, expanding product lines, and building customer affinity. Vista is a manufacturer, not a retailer. Stores like REI, where consumers come in to look at and hopefully purchase products, are a big deal to their success.

And these consumers, all of which are human beings, follow the news and have strong beliefs.

In February of 2018, a gunman in Parkland, Florida, shot

34 people, killing 17 at Stoneman Douglas High School. In the wake of this horrific event, REI discovered that Vista was not just manufacturing CamelBaks—they were also manufacturing gun components and ammunition.

One of REI's main beliefs is to enjoy nature and life while still preserving both. That means if you walk into a sacred space like the Grand Canyon, you take out everything you brought in with you. At REI, they take it seriously and equip customers with the knowledge and products to take it seriously, too.

After Parkland, the senior leaders at REI considered what they knew about Vista and gave them a choice: You can either stop making gun components and ammunition, or you can no longer have us as a client—we'll stop selling CamelBaks, your bike helmets, etc.

Choose.

REI clearly realized that selling and buying CamelBaks has nothing to do with guns, but the point was deeper: Vista didn't believe what REI believes.

Vista continued to make their gun components and ammunition, and REI walked away from one of its biggest suppliers. They drew a hard line in the sand and stuck to who they were and what they believed at the core. In fact, on March 1, 2018, here's exactly what REI posted on their own website about the decision:

This morning we learned that Vista does not plan to make a public statement that outlines a clear plan of action. As a result, we have decided to place a hold on future orders of products that Vista sells through REI while we assess how Vista proceeds.

Companies are showing they can contribute if they are willing to lead. We encourage Vista to do just that.

I've got to tell you, I love this. I applaud REI and their willingness to alienate people as they stand up for what they believe in. And remember, Vista creates a product I need. One I've purchased and will likely need to purchase again. But I don't care. Bring me a knockoff, because I'm with REI on this one.

Think about it: The people who come into REI stores are outdoorsmen. Many of them probably own a gun, and for REI to take umbrage with the notion of making gun components and ammunition is incredible. REI made a choice to value human life over profits, and I, for one, applaud them.

More importantly, I'll shop there more! Because REI believes what I believe, I'll find reasons to shop there for clothes, shoes...maybe a kayak or a big tent. You know, outdoor stuff.

Remember, your choices will inevitably alienate people. That's a good thing. If you lose business for shouting what you believe, you'll be rewarded on the other side. Those are your people. They are more loyal because they know what you believe, and they'll latch onto you for it.

UNFOUNDED FEAR

It's actually an unfounded fear that you'll lose business and alienate potential customers by standing for something. Roughly equal to the number of people you piss off, there will be a similar number of people who are excited to work with you.

There's not a single company on the planet—not even Amazon—that has the capacity to do everything for everyone. You just can't—nobody has enough time and bandwidth. What's more fun is working with a small group of people who believe what you believe and alienating those who don't.

You create congruence. There are some clients I've had where no matter how well we serve them, what we charge them, who works on their project, and no matter what we do, there's just friction. It just doesn't work right.

Then there are others that even if we go over budget and miss deadlines, it's like a warm knife through room-temperature butter. It's just easy!

They give you wiggle room. That's a side effect of shouting what you believe and attracting people who believe what you do—it makes projects frictionless.

> The wisest sages of business teach the power of "no." Say no to all sorts of things, and only say yes to the things that fit your core beliefs: your way of being and thinking.

THE BIGGEST FINANCIAL FIRM IN PADUCAH, KENTUCKY

You won't see the city of Paducah, Kentucky, on the front page of *The Wall Street Journal* anytime soon. It's not exactly what you'd call a hotbed of financial activity. It's a tiny little flyover town in a part of the world nobody thinks about.

Not a lot of guys are flying private Gulfstream jets into Paducah, you know what I mean?

But Keith Jennings, the owner of his eponymous financial firm in Paducah, has managed to do something amazing in that little town. He's taken a stand to help educate his clients on what financial wellness actually looks like, rather than sell them some financial products they won't truly benefit from. He wants his clients to look at money in a new way and have open conversations. He punches the entire financial services industry in the face and is willing to wear a badge that says he's not like everybody else. He doesn't care how much you have to invest, he just cares about *you*.

He's the financial advisor who often plays the part of therapist, marriage counselor, priest, and shoulder to cry on for his clients.

He worked with one couple that had been married for twenty-five years. The wife thought it was most secure to keep their money in stacks of hundreds in a box under their bed. The husband said they should put the money in the stock market. It was a constant rub between the two of them for *twenty-five years*. It was a huge, underlying problem that put a real strain on their marriage.

What Keith does is educate in a way that helps people like this get synced up before they do anything else. He doesn't say, "Let's use this finance vehicle or that tax shelter." He educates on the deeper meaning of money, on what it means in their lives, and he knows that it's not for everybody.

Anyone can go to the budget online brokerages like E*TRADE or Charles Schwab; Keith even tells you about those options! But people come to Keith for something different: real financial education.

He alienates a lot of people accustomed to the status quo, but he's also created one heck of a following. Oh sure, most of his clients are in his local geography, but not everyone. Word has spread, and in the process of shouting his beliefs, he's drawn in clients from around the country—all of whom need his services, and all of whom believe what he believes.

MERRELL SHOES: IN OR OUT?

Imagine watching two people working out, side by side on a television screen. On the left, the fit woman walks into the gym and jumps onto the treadmill. You see close-ups of her shoes and hear the whirr of the treadmill. On the right side of the screen is a man running across dirt trails, past marker posts, and over rocky boulders out into the woods.

The woman on the left steps off the treadmill, wipes her face, and hops into the shower. The man on the right side takes off his shirt and jumps into a mountain stream.

Then a question is posed in big white letters on the screen: "In or out?"

That's a summary of a spectacular online ad for Merrell

Shoes, the outdoor athletic shoe brand. What's cool is that there's no judgment in the advertisement. If you like going to the gym and running in the air conditioning with headphones in, more power to you. Go grab some Nikes.

But if you're an outdoors person who gets muddy, jumps through trails, and traipses through the woods, you should buy Merrell Shoes.

Merrell fully discloses what they believe, without being judgmental. And they designed their shoe line to reflect that ruggedness.

And speaking of Nike...

I've talked about the Nike brand a number of times in this book, but I, like many people, had no specific affinity for Nike. That is until a moment in 2018 when former NFL quarterback Colin Kaepernick was featured in a Nike ad that referred to his kneeling protests.

The copy in the ad left no room for gray, it was black and white: "Believe in something. Even if it means sacrificing everything." Nike made a calculated decision; they knew people would vehemently disagree with their beliefs. In response, a lot of people burned shoes, cut Nike logos off apparel, and destroyed equipment like golf clubs and tennis rackets. "Screw Nike!" they said.

It was perhaps the most American moment of my life.

Sure, you could say that Nike made a decision based on data that showed there were more Nike wearers who supported Colin Kaepernick than not, and that may be true—but they've also chosen to be bold throughout their history. For example, when companies dropped Tiger Woods during his affair scandal, Nike stuck with him. They champion outliers—that's just who they are.

I love that. So while some were burning, I was buying. Literally the next day, my wife and I went and each bought a new pair of Nike shoes, and new Nike shirts with giant swooshes on them. We intentionally went for a walk in our neighborhood, sporting our new gear, with the intention of telling the world what we believe. If people want to talk to me about it, that's fine. And if others don't like it, they don't have to call me—we don't need to be friends or work together.

It's not about passing judgment on others. It's about trying to work with people who are congruent with you and your beliefs. It may seem risky, but it's actually better for you and your company. But at the same time...

DON'T SCREAM JUST TO SCREAM

There's no reason to be an ass and instigate fights. Lots of people in my world (even people I'm extremely close to) don't agree with Colin Kaepernick and Nike. That means they don't agree with me!

That doesn't mean we're going to engage in fisticuffs. In fact, my relationship with my business partner is stronger because we can engage in civil, level-headed discussions on topics we disagree on. This one included.

This is about trying to make a difference by uncovering our core beliefs and codifying them so they're accessible to you, your employees, and your customers.

You're not for everyone. And that's a good thing.

REI didn't seek out a gun controversy, and they didn't try to find some moral high ground on the gun issue. They just saw something related to their core beliefs bubble to the surface in the social unconscious, and they chose to act in congruence with their beliefs.

They simply stuck to their guns, and so should you...and, of course, I only mean that metaphorically.

CHAPTER 10

BREAK FROM THE HERD AND SHOUT YOUR WHY

"Dream big and be disruptive. If you are doing the same thing as everyone else, you've already failed."

—KENDRA SCOTT

Back in 1955, *Fortune Magazine* started its "Fortune 500," an annual list of the 500 biggest companies in America. Do you know how many of these iconic titans of industry made the list in **both** 1955 and 2018?

Fifty-four. That's it. That means of the original 500, 446 no longer exist—and these were, at that time, the biggest, coolest, most cutting-edge companies in America!

Remember those buffalo from the Introduction, the ones that followed one another over the edge of the cliff to their death? Those are the companies no longer on the Fortune 500 list. And unfortunately, it's almost every organization out there. Don't be a buffalo. Break from the herd and embrace a clearly articulated core belief and shout it with abandon.

Now, tap the brakes, please. Don't come after me with a pitchfork or a hockey stick. I get it. I've followed the herd plenty of times in my life. Why? Because it's hard not to! And like you, I'm human. In an effort to stand out, grow our business, attract top talent, and get new clients, sometimes I've followed the well-worn path instead of a brand-new one.

I deeply believe, however, that if you adopt the herd mentality, you'll be in trouble. That's the key here. What's especially challenging is that following the status quo is not actually an awful strategy—there's a reason it exists as a natural phenomenon.

But being part of a herd poses another problem: You don't share your gifts with the world.

$901 BILLION—WHO CARES?

When I lived in Chicago, I was one of the herd commuting to the office, moving in and out of the city to the suburbs every day. For decades, I did a reverse commute—

meaning I lived in the heart of the city, but drove to the outlying suburbs to my office. Every day, I battled gridlock and boredom on the freeway. This isn't a beautiful drive, either. In fact, it's littered with the infrastructure of industry and enormous billboards up and down both sides of the roadway.

One day, just a few exits from my office, I noticed a billboard and couldn't believe it. It was an ad for Prudential, and it featured their well-known slogan, "Get a piece of the rock."

The large, rocky outcropping prominently displayed in their logo is the Rock of Gibraltar, guarding passage into the Mediterranean Sea. It's been a stoic, impervious land mass associated with military strength for centuries. Prudential wants all of us (the consumer) to associate our financial well-being with this same rock-solid security.

The first time I drove by this billboard, I was probably going damn near 80 mph so I doubt I noticed it. But after a few more days, I absolutely knew the billboard. In fact, I knew it so well that I went a little off the deep end.

Really, I did.

I remember getting into the office and pitching quite a fit. I huffed and puffed to anyone who would listen. Of course, I found this billboard to be reprehensible, caustic, boorish, clumsy, and, worst of all, selfish.

It was so terrible that it actually provided fodder for training programs I wrote long before this book. Of course, I just had to snap a picture:

You're welcome. That's right, I risked life and limb getting this picture, pulling my car over on the expressway with semi-trucks and other vehicles whipping by at 80 mph. I could have died, you know.

Boasting that you have more than $901 billion in assets under management is selfish. That phrase only tells us about them. As a consumer, you immediately wonder how you fit into that equation. I mean, even the richest person on the planet doesn't come close to that kind of wealth.

But what do I have? Pocket change compared to that. It made me feel small and belittled as a consumer, like I have nothing they would want. I wanted them to tell me what I would get from those assets. How do I benefit?

What's in it for me? It's really hard to see how I, Joe Average, can fit into that behemoth of a business.

All of this got me thinking...hey, Prudential, with all those billions, do you have the best people in the business?

The best products and services?

The best technology?

It was a 901 billion-pound gorilla on the interstate, and I had no answer.

CLARITY OVER CLEVERNESS

You don't need to be overly clever with your messaging, as long as you're explicit about your belief. Be clear, codify it, then scream it.

Tell me what you stand for, not how big your bank balance is.

I fixed the Prudential billboard. No, I didn't grab my can of spray paint and hop a barbed-wire fence to vandalize the billboard (although, now that I think of that, I wish I had). No, I asked my team of talented designers to edit the photo. This time, it's all about focusing on the customer.

See the difference? Actually, can you *feel* the difference? That *feel*, right there, is what this whole book is all about.

How much do you care if I tell you our corporate headquarters is 2,400 square feet, we've got 10 employees, and every computer we use is a state-of-the-art Mac? Big deal. But if I tell you we're going to "make waves," elevating everything you do so people remember and act on your messages, then yeah, you'll respond to that.

It's clever, sure, but it's also deeply authentic. And you can do anything proudly and loudly if it's authentic.

I have an uncle, Uncle Barry, who's the most genuine, authentic person I know. From the outside, you'd see an Indiana good ol' boy by way of Central Florida. But don't judge this book by its cover. Uncle Barry is smart—wicked smart. He can instantly read a room; the guy has incredible emotional intelligence. And IQ points? Oh yeah, my Uncle Barry is deep. He knows about all kinds of things from world history and national politics to medicine and sports.

His intelligence is very real, but it's also hidden under a heavy veil of Wrangler jeans, plaid shirts, cigarette smoke, and talk of his truck, hot coffee, BBQ rub, or tool shed. Come to think of it, it's usually a combination of all four at the same time.

The most amazing thing about my uncle is how deeply comfortable he is with the life choices he's made. He's a former firefighter, and now sells flooring for a small business owner that's half-son, half-brother to him. Alongside my adorable aunt JoJo, he's got everything he wants or needs. He doesn't desire to see or do much more than he's been doing, and he could truly care less about your opinion of him. Uncle Barry has always been and will always be his own man, no matter what, for better or worse, take it or leave it.

That is not an easy position to take.

Certainly most people, and without question most organizations, care deeply about other people's opinions. Just look at the very genuine desire that so many people have for "likes" on Instagram or Facebook. Generally speaking, as humans and as companies, we want to be affirmed by those around us.

Authenticity isn't easy. It's being able to find true comfort in your own skin, and that means in your own beliefs. It means following the example set by individuals like my uncle who fully understand the choices, consequences, and outcomes of everything they do.

You might fully understand your core beliefs, but do you possess the necessary bravery to live authentically? To build a business authentically?

CONCLUSION

THE ADVENTURE IS WORTH IT

Once you figure out your core beliefs, you have a respon-sibility. Seriously, you have no choice—you have to get out there. You owe it to yourself and the world to stand for something. It would be disingenuous to hold back once you know what lies underneath your actions. You aren't serving yourself, your customers, or your employees if you keep your beliefs deep and hidden. You have to be bold, and that starts right now.

BEAUTY, LOVE, AND ADVENTURE

My wife is a psychotherapist and executive coach, so she has an incredibly unique view on life. She lives her life in a way that consciously seeks out beauty, love, and adventure in all things. The beauty might be the leaves of a tree in autumn, or the stars in the sky, or the architecture of a home. Love might be when a stranger picks up a dropped wallet and returns it. Adventure might mean taking surfing lessons or trying the new Thai restaurant in your neighborhood.

Beauty, love, and adventure can take a lot of different forms.

I'm going to tell you right now—leading with your beliefs is an adventure worth doing. It's a wild ride, and you may hit some moments where you can't find the beauty or love anywhere. But it's worth it, I promise. You'll feel a connection to your life, your work, and your people in a bigger, better way. You'll actually love them!

The risk is big, but the reward is even bigger.

PUT THIS BOOK DOWN

Immediately after reading this conclusion, I want you to get to work!

Assuming you now know what you stand for, have you done the simple stuff like change your outgoing voicemail message?

Have you changed the signature line on your email?

Have you thought through what your new business cards should say?

Start there, then keep going. Expand your efforts over time.

If you work at a company and you now realize they don't believe what you believe, put the book down and work on your résumé. Then, I challenge you to scour the planet to find an organization that's perfect for you. Not based on job description or positions you've had in the past, but rather on shared beliefs.

If you can find a place that fits what you believe—it doesn't matter what the job is—it won't feel like work at all, and it will be worth every ounce of effort you've put into it.

Life is too *long* to do anything other than what matters most to you.

Remember that Subaru commercial from the Introduction—the most valuable real estate on Earth?

For you, it's not the backseat of a Subaru. The most valuable real estate on Earth for you are the places in your heart and mind that hold your core beliefs.

Own that real estate and speak from that place, and you will be unstoppable.

Sometimes it's impossible to read the label from inside the jar. If you're stuck and can't figure it out, shoot us an email at info@squareplanet.com. We'd love to hear from you, and we'd be glad to help.

ACKNOWLEDGMENTS

I'd like to start by simply saying "thanks" to my immediate family, those most aware and routinely affected (positively and negatively) by my rather strong opinions: Mom, Dad, Kelly, John, Michael, Matt, Ethan, Janie, Mike, Sherry, Jean-Jean the Dancing Machine, Lisha, Joe, Noah, Josie, and my whole gaggle of aunts, uncles, and cousins! I've learned so much from all of you. Thank you for everything.

My uncles, Mitch and Barry, and Jim Palmer who I consider family, the three of you helped me become a better man, person, husband, and business owner. I'm deeply grateful. You probably didn't know it at the time, but the wisdom in your words and actions throughout my life have mattered a great deal to me. Your core beliefs were continually on display and that was a powerful influence. Thank you for being awesome in so many ways.

To my business partners, Brian Jansen and Paul Fehren-bacher, guys, you are the best. Thank you for your support, friendship, patience, and forgiveness. Bri, there was a time when we were on the fence about this. Thankfully we got it right! I respect you and trust you implicitly; I'm excited about our journey ahead. Paul, you always make me think deeper than I would have on my own. You've pushed me to dream big, and I know our best is yet to come. Guys, I love you and think of you as brothers; I'd probably even give you a kidney. Maybe. Thanks for everything.

This is not an exaggeration: The ridiculous life I enjoy today never would have come to be without Doug Carter, Kaylee Conrad, Maxx Parcell, Kim Chua, Derek Rudel, Frank Wandersee, Tim Eisenbrandt, and JoAnn Auster.

Doug, your fingerprints will always be on SQP. Thank you for so many building blocks laid into the foundation. You did that, and you're more appreciated than you know.

Kaylee and Maxx, your words, keen insights, and creative ideas can be found on every page of this book. I hope you'll look back and feel our time together was one of the true highlights of your careers. I can tell you, it's absolutely one of mine. Thank you both for everything!

Kim, Derek, Frank, and Tim, you are all amazing. Way

more than amazing employees, you are amazing people. My life is better because you've been in it, and I simply can't thank you enough for all your help. One thing that would make me happy: a group pic in your Nikes.

And JoJo, part mom, part voice of reason, part trusted advisor; you've done it all. Thank you for being the consistent, powerful, steadying force through it all.

There is a long list of incredible professional relationships that have influenced me and the content within this book. In no particular order, huge thanks to Jason DeSanto, Raman Chadha, Catherine Jelinek, Mike Marasco, Stig Nybo, Jessica Wells, Nancy DePaolo, Pete Allen, Barbara Wiest, John Timmerman, Simon Sinek, Ashley Page, Robbie Abed, Dan Ptak, Seth Kravitz, Bruce Sirus, Art Massa, Dave McCreery, Mike Maddock, Joe Tortorich, Scott Roberts, Tom Tomchak, Linda Dao, Drew McCullough, Kelly Manthey, Tom LaMantia, Kelli "Renfro" Myers, and Steve Koppel. All of you helped me work out the kinks, develop the formula, and grow as a person. My appreciation can't be measured.

Special thanks to all the individuals and organizations noted inside this book. Your participation was not only crucial, but fun. The opportunity to work with all of you has been the highlight of my career.

And to those incredible people who penned "back cover

blurbs"...I owe you big time. Thank you for being awesome. You raised my confidence and enthusiasm, much appreciated!

I must honor the thousands of audience members who've participated in my live keynote presentations. Thank you for allowing me to present these ideas as I worked out the nuances of my message. Your time, attention, and patience are deeply appreciated.

Special thanks to the entire team at Scribe Media, especially Karla Bynum, Greg Larson, Bailey Hayes, Cindy Curtis, Erin Tyler, and Julie Arends.

To my deeply loyal, loving, and encouraging friends who didn't tease me when I said I was going to write a business book. Brian Mohr, Jackie Mohr, Cathy Carroll, Ken Anderson, Jason Crane, Mike Walsh, Dan Close, Jeff Israel, Eric Boyd, Dave Dyson, and Chris Hibbard, you all rock. I expect to see a copy of this book on your shelf for a very long time, signed of course. You're all amazing and I love you.

Mike and Sherry, you've consistently helped in ways that don't always get acknowledged. That generosity and encouragement have fueled so many things, including an adventurous spirit that I sorely needed. From water skiing to surfing to running businesses, you two have provided expertise, love, counsel, and support to make things happen. I'm so lucky to get you for in-laws; I love you and I thank you.

I've always said my work is half art, half science. Dad, thanks for the art. Mom, thanks for the science. Without your incredible support from Day 1, there is no chance I'd get to this station in life. With encouragement and help, love and discipline, you raised me to dream, ask tough questions, act confidently, strive for answers, and explore different paths. Interestingly, the first place I realized I could "stand for something" was in our own home. While we certainly didn't always agree, I'm deeply appreciative of your willingness to listen. I owe so much to both of you; Mom and Dad, thanks for everything, I love you very deeply.

Shawna, in a book full of words, I simply can't find enough of them to express how much I love you. What a difference three minutes can make, right? You are the very best thing that has ever happened to me, the absolute most amazing part of my life. You're my girl, and I'm the luckiest man alive to have found you. Your encouragement and counsel have been incredibly important; seriously, I can't imagine all of this without you. My love for you knows no boundary and I thank you for quite literally everything, because with you as my partner, every dream has already come true.

ABOUT THE AUTHOR

 Brian believes in making waves. For the record, these are not waves of the aquatic variety. He's the founder and Chief Word Guy at SquarePlanet Presentations & Strategy, a Phoenix, Arizona-based business communications firm. He's also the co-founder and co-owner of AlterEgoAV and Mutt Jackson, both based in Chicago, Illinois.

Brian is also an adjunct lecturer at Northwestern University's Farley Center for Entrepreneurship and Innovation. He's a highly sought-after speaker, presenting regularly to audiences around the globe about core beliefs and the inherent power of communication.

He has decades of experience as a leader across a wide

range of creative industries, including one-on-one coaching with C-suite leaders at Fortune 500 companies, TED speakers, *Shark Tank* contestants, and countless business owners, helping them communicate and lead how they've always imagined. He's worked with some of the biggest brands in the world, including Coca-Cola, Red Bull, Google, Citibank, Jim Beam, Northern Trust, Redbox, United Airlines, General Motors, and more.

He loves the Chicago Bears and is eternally optimistic about them going 19-0. Yes, that's a perfect season, inclusive of the Super Bowl. He's an obnoxious food snob and a lousy ceramic artist. He moved away from the frozen tundra of Chicago to live in Arizona with his amazing wife, Shawna, to enjoy hikes, sunsets, hummingbirds, and perfect weather. Visitors are welcome and encouraged.

APPENDIX

One manifestation of shouting out loud is through your recruiting and hiring process. The best organizations know that culture fits make all the difference. The way you get the right people is to lead with beliefs in your job postings.

AN EXAMPLE OF ONE OF OUR JOB POSTINGS

At SquarePlanet, we believe in making waves. We also believe in the implicit power of a great story. And we know that a picture really is worth a thousand words. We think presentations are amazing opportunities, not tasks that undoubtedly suck the life out of a room. We're looking for fine craftsmen, but don't let the colloquial nature of the term fool you: non-males please apply.

We're looking for another pirate to join our cause and propel the business of business communications forward. And this isn't the Horn of Africa or Johnny Depp kind of pirate, no. This is the break the rules, take risks, think different, Steve Jobs, kind of pirate.

We typically rebuke the well-worn path, but we're not rebellious without cause. We believe art is what moves the world and stirs the soul. And we know that artists, and true masters of the arts, exist in a myriad of forms. Our methods have already had a remarkable effect on many notable brands, but that doesn't mean we're a great fit for every suitor.

SquarePlanet is on the prowl for an art director/chief designer extraordinaire. You will be the leader of a small team with a mission to help visualize stories that make the complex simple, the ugly beautiful, and the boring bold. We exist to help our clients' most important messages be easily understood, remembered, and acted upon.

We make presentations that matter.

We produce conferences and events that engage and educate.

We teach skills that elevate people and performances.

Your role is to proactively lead your team in crafting the "oooohs and ahhhhhs" our clients have come to expect. In fact, if you think this role is about making slides or simply designing a PowerPoint deck, please move on to the next job posting, SquarePlanet isn't for you. But if you're the kind of designer who loves developing unique, engaging ways to transform the benign to the bodacious, keep reading. Make no mistake: You're gonna make a lot of PowerPoint decks, but these are a very long way from the typical.

You'll need to be a consummate professional. We believe that all members of our team, as well as our clients, treat each other with honesty, respect, and compassion. We believe the work we do and the manner in which we do it must always be rich in responsibility and fairness.

You should have a strong desire to follow our protocol and

procedure. But you're expected to speak up if you know a better way. You should be thrilled to jump in and help, knowing your greatest responsibility is actually to your fellow employees first.

You know how to find the perfect balance between speed and quality. You are a lifelong learner. You are open to ideas, open to collaboration, and OK with not always getting your way.

Sometimes we work too many hours in a row. Sometimes we struggle to fill the idle time. Sometimes we work in cold ballrooms at large convention hotels in places like Las Vegas and Orlando. Sometimes we work at home, on a company-supplied laptop, in our PJs. We work an honest day and we're not thrilled with results that are anything less than jaw-dropping.

You'd be a great candidate if you hit the traits below, in no particular order:

1. You have experience leading a design team. We're in search of someone to help steer the ship, but it's less important than attitude. We're keen on sunny, personable people who understand the needs to be proactive, organized, and obsessed with moving projects forward. Negative Nancy or Sullen Sam need not apply.

2. It's nonnegotiable/mission critical for you to possess deep knowledge and skills in the Adobe Creative Suite, PowerPoint, and Apple Keynote. Motion graphics knowledge is big. Very big. HUGE. REALLY HUGE.

3. You can effectively communicate with team members and clients. That means a certain maturity and confidence. It means you are able to write a cogent email, speak on the phone professionally, and carry yourself in-person like a true pro. It means the use of emojis, Snapchat, and Instagram are not your best methods of communicating.

4. You know how to juggle. Lots of projects, lots of timelines. You need to be able to effectively divide and conquer assignments within the team, as well as collaborate on the overall creative of every project. OK, you don't really need to know how to juggle, you just need to be able to handle various tasks, personalities, and deadlines at a single time. But frankly, it wouldn't hurt your chances if you could actually juggle. Just sayin'.

5. Are you a slower learner? Need long hours to digest material for full comprehension? Is your spirit animal a desert tortoise? Does the mere notion of a Crock-Pot put a smile on your face? Yeah, you're gonna struggle here.

6. Mistakes happen, after all you're human. (You ARE human, right?) It's how you recover that matters. We expect people to make BIG mistakes, not little ones. Seriously. Spell a client's name wrong = very, very bad. Delete the whole server of every existing asset we've ever created = so catastrophic that we'd laugh. Point is, we're not expecting perfect, but we are looking for professionals who care about the work and the approach taken around that work.

7. You effectively utilize the biologically driven ratio of two ears and one mouth. This means you listen more than you talk. Our founder is the notable exception to this rule and it is what it is.

8. You've been exposed to corporate meetings and events. The majority of the work we do is in direct support of conferences. While not a deal-breaker, any knowledge, even cursory, of this side of our business is helpful.

9. Desire to join a company built around great culture and great work. SquarePlanet enjoys an enviable client list of world-class brands that contract us to provide high-value work in a timely, professional manner. The expectation is that all employees fit that same mold.

10. You live in the Valley of the Sun. SquarePlanet's world-wide megaplex is located just off SR51 and Glendale Ave., in the geographic "center" of the valley. The expected norm is to work in the office on a regular basis.

The Basic Requirements

Bachelor's degree in Graphic Design or other similar field from a respected school. Actual experience, think 6-10 years of relevant work experience as a Production Artist / Production Designer / Lead Designer / Art Director with a compelling portfolio you're excited to share.

Mac person, but capable in Windows.

Jedi master of Adobe CS applications plus PowerPoint and Keynote.

You don't smell like dirty shoes.

Able to professionally express yourself with written and verbal communication skills.

True self-starter. Not our job to write your to-do list every day.

A nice person, who people generally like. Sorry, your nana doesn't count.

Willingness to travel on a somewhat regular basis.

SquarePlanet offers a competitive salary, healthcare benefits, a 401(k)-retirement package, a generous PTO policy, nine paid holidays, a pair of custom Nike shoes upon your one-year anniversary, a truly congenial, collaborative, and professional work environment, copious amounts of creative freedom, and a client list you'd be proud to be associated with.